VEGETARIAN BARBECUE

80 EASY-TO-GRILL RECIPES INCLUDING DIPS, SKEWERS, SALADS AND SIDES

VEGETARIAN BARBECUE

80 EASY-TO-GRILL RECIPES INCLUDING DIPS, SKEWERS, SALADS AND SIDES

ROSS DOBSON

HarperCollins*Publishers*Ltd

CONTENTS

INTRODUCTION

When looking for vegetarian recipes for inspiration, you really don't have to search too hard: Next time you are at your local South-East Asian, Chinese, Indian, Japanese, or Middle Eastern restaurant, have a closer look at the menu. These cultures have long traditions of vegetarianism, so naturally their cuisines are loaded with wonderful vegetarian dishes, featuring ingredients that are now more easily accessible than ever before.

I happen to be Australian, and in Australia we do love our grills. And many vegetarian dishes from afar are indeed perfectly suited to grilling. But I must be a little careful here, as this is no more an Australian cookbook than it is a cookbook just for vegetarians.

Vegetarian grill cookery is not about trying to reinvent the wheel. And good vegetarian cooking is certainly not about a need to make a meat substitute. Some vegetarian dishes stand alone as marvels in their own right. The famous Middle Eastern eggplant dip known as baba ghanoush, for instance, simply cannot be made without a good lick from a naked flame. This purplish black vegetable (well, actually, it's a fruit) withstands the searing heat of the grill, while the flesh inside cooks to a silky, smoke-infused softness.

Or how about grilled onion rings, which often start off the grill because they take some time to slowly cook to a soft, golden, caramelized sweetness, filling the air with a mouthwatering fug, while also seasoning the hotplate nicely, ready to flavor the next batch of grilled food. Grilled onions are good enough to eat on their own, but toss them warm, into a bowl with a twist of lemon juice, some soy sauce, and mirin and you have something pretty special without too much effort.

And don't forget the humble potato cooked in its own skin. Large potatoes are best left unpeeled, wrapped in foil and cooked on the grill until the flesh inside is pillow soft, ready to be cut open and filled with butter, sour cream, or labneh, and finished off with a sprinkling of salt and some soft herbs like parsley, chervil, tarragon, or chives.

There is something magically atmospheric about the hiss of food on the grill and the irresistible aromas that accompany it. This is quick, simple cooking at its sizzling best.

Take the famous Jemaa el-Fna market, held in a large, medieval square in Marrakesh. By day it is a thriving maze of market goods, selling everything from orange juice to leather backpacks, with snake charmers, charlatans, and magicians vying for attention. At night it transforms, in my mind, into the world's largest grill. Hundreds of food stalls are lit up by blurred fairy lights, made even

more romantic by the thick shroud of barbecue smoke in the air. So special is this place that it has been proclaimed a UNESCO Masterpiece of the Oral and Intangible Heritage of Humanity.

The Aw Taw Kaw market in Bangkok is similarly famous for its smoking woks and hotplates, sizzling with grilled treats. Here, the metal skewers of the Middle Eastern kebab give way to bamboo skewers, and I have included plenty of recipes for both styles of kebab in this book.

Tender vine vegetables such as small heirloom tomatoes, zucchini, and eggplant are naturally skewerable. You can skewer just about any vegetable you like, although do remember to partly cook harder root vegetables beforehand, to give them a chance to cook through. Skewered vegetables like big flavors, so alternate them with cubes of firm cheese such as haloumi or Indian paneer. Cook until the cheese is golden and the vegetables tender, then finish off with some herbs and a tangy citrus-based dressing.

I use my new grill as an oven of sorts. Most modern grills have lids and mine, with its stainless steel encasing, conducts and radiates heat really well. When cooking breads, and for nicely charred vegetables and cheese, preheat the grill and hotplate burners to high and close the lid. You will see the thermometer rise and the grill will then act like an oven. You can sit a cooking rack on the hotplate or rack, keeping food off the direct heat, to make the most perfect and authentic breads; in particular it's a great way to cook pocket bread. (The lid of the grill, by the way, is also a great spot to prove bread dough.) But don't stress if your grill doesn't have a lid — an upturned metal mixing bowl will do the same job.

And do use all those inventions of convenience in your kitchen as well. Cook saucy things in little heatproof pots directly on the grill. Tear off a sheet of parchment paper to cook the food on, especially soft ingredients like tomatoes and cheese — your food will still have appetizing grill marks, but without the mess, and the corners of the paper can be used to pick up the cooked food and tumble it into a bowl or straight onto a platter. Wrap food in foil or parchment paper to make parcels that are steamed within; for an air of added drama, these grilled parcels can be served and unwrapped at the table.

Choose quality, seasonally fresh ingredients, stick to the classic flavor combinations, introduce a variation or two to keep things interesting and you can't go wrong. If you are even remotely familiar with vegetarian cooking, you'll know this already. And if not, after tasting some of the recipes in this book, you'll hopefully agree that vegetarian cookery definitely deserves a place on the grill.

9

TYPES OF GRILLS

Compared to other foods, cooking vegetarian recipes on the grill involves relatively little mess and little smoke, which offers greater flexibility. Still, when testing the recipes in my grill books, I usually do so on my old front porch, so I can make as much mess and smoke as I need to.

I often find myself developing recipes in winter, and because of deadlines I can't always wait for the sun to shine before I start grilling. The great thing about the vegetarian recipes in this book is that in wet or cold weather you can simply cook them inside on an electric grill or hotplate! But this is really defeating the social nature of grilling, so I'm assuming for this book that you will generally be cooking outdoors.

Here are the main pros and cons for the different contraptions you can use.

ELECTRIC

Electric grills offer a mobile and convenient way of cooking, and are ideal for apartment living. Even better if you have a deck, so you feel like you are grilling outdoors. But they do have downsides: electric grills often have a built-in thermostat that cuts out the heat, meaning you have less control when cooking. Not ideal when grilling.

GAS

Cooking with gas gives you excellent control over the heat, which is what a good grill is all about. However, with a gas grill, you can never cook using LPG indoors; the other issue is making sure you actually have gas to burn, and topping up the LPG tank is not always convenient or inexpensive. Some outdoor grills have the luxury of gas piped directly into them.

WOOD

Wood grills require attention, but are fun to use and produce a barbecued result like no other. Maintaining the heat is tricky and it will take time to master a wood-fired grill. They are ideal in the great outdoors and in a big backyard. But because they are generally constructed of brick, they aren't at all mobile, which is an obvious limitation.

CHARCOAL

Charcoal grills are designed as compact, mobile units, which equates to convenience. They range in size and function, with many of the larger charcoal grills designed to slow-cook big cuts of meat. Like gas grills, they obviously cannot be used indoors, but are great if you have a backyard or even a small deck.

In Japan, what we know as a hibachi was actually designed to heat homes, not to cook with. In America the hibachi grill has become synonymous with quick, efficient, and healthy grilling.

Smaller charcoal grills can actually be placed in the center of the table, making the grilling experience very interactive.

DIPS & BITS

What often makes a grill memorable are all those extra things. The things we often see and taste first, all ready to go, set up at the table. Some we try to forget, like a tub of sour cream mixed up with dehydrated French onion soup and given the title "French onion dip." Remember that beauty? While this is not what I call cooking, it is the stuff of memories.

And how often do you hear "that was the best dip," "what was in that sauce?" or "I must have the recipe for that dressing!"?

It doesn't really matter what it is, it comes back to the same thing: The experience that is sharing. I have found that if the scene is set for a lovely, relaxed day, or night, the enjoyment of the food is enhanced. I wonder if this explains our love of a grill. Or when we say the very word "barbecue" we think a sunny day, party, celebration, fun.

Most of the recipes here make use of the grill. Except for a few salad dressings, I think it is essential that the grill be used at some stage of the recipe. If you have the space, the time and the weather permits, why not make the whole thing grill-side? Peel and mash the sweet squash, sprinkle a mixture of Arabian spices over just-hot flatbread, swirl golden corn through sour cream, or have a guest stir the fresh salsa ingredients together.

SQUASH, BLACK BEAN, & FETA DIP

Serves 8–10

1 butternut squash,
    about 3 lb 5 oz
2 tablespoons olive oil
1 teaspoon ground cumin
½ teaspoon cayenne pepper
14 oz can black beans,
    rinsed and well drained
3½ oz feta cheese, crumbled
½ cup chopped cilantro leaves
    and stalks
½ teaspoon sea salt
extra virgin olive oil, for drizzling
chargrilled bread, to serve

This dip is a cinch. You take one really nice-looking squash and cook it on the grill until the skin is blackened — for about an hour, give or take. There is no strict timing here, it depends on the size and shape of the squash. The inspiration came from my "Barbie" Ghanoush recipe, where the eggplant is kept whole and simply cooked on a grill. That recipe is on page 25. Check it out.

Preheat the grill to medium.

Sit the squash on the grill and close the lid, if you have one, or cover with a metal bowl. Cook for about an hour, turning often until the skin of the squash is blackened all over. Remove the squash from the grill and allow to cool slightly.

When cool enough to handle, peel the tough skin off the squash and discard it. Cut the squash lengthways down the middle and scoop out the seeds.

Roughly chop the flesh of the squash and place in a large bowl. Add the olive oil, cumin, cayenne pepper, beans, feta, cilantro, and salt and use a fork to combine. Drizzle with extra virgin olive oil and serve with chargrilled bread.

NOTE: This dip will keep in an airtight container in the fridge for 2–3 days.

14

**VEGETARIAN
BARBECUE**

CHIMICHURRI

Chimichurri is an Argentinian salsa verde or, simply put, green sauce. But this herbaceous green sauce is more rugged than its European counterparts. Some say chimichurri should taste like it has been dragged through the herb garden, and that's a pretty good description.

1 large, ripe tomato
4 scallions
4 garlic cloves, unpeeled
6 cups roughly chopped flat-leaf parsley
2 cups chopped cilantro leaves and stalks
½ teaspoon dried Greek oregano (see Notes)
½ teaspoon sea salt
¼ cup olive oil
¼ cup white wine vinegar
chargrilled potato wedges, to serve (see Notes)

Preheat the grill to high.

Place the tomato, scallions, and garlic on the grill. Use metal tongs to turn the vegetables until the skins are charred — almost blackened — all over. Remove from the heat and allow to cool.

When cool enough to handle, peel the vegetables and garlic and discard the charred skins. Don't be too fussy about removing all the skins — they'll add a smoky flavor to the chimichurri.

Place all the vegetables and the garlic in a food processor and blitz until finely chopped. Add the herbs, oregano, and salt and pulse to combine.

With the motor running, add the oil, then the vinegar, to make a smooth sauce.

Serve with chargrilled potato wedges as a dip, or spoon over chargrilled eggplant.

NOTES: The chimichurri will keep in an airtight container in the fridge for 2–3 days.

For this recipe I prefer to use Greek oregano, sold in bunches with the leaves and stems still intact. It is sweeter and somehow less medicinal tasting than the prepackaged stuff.

To chargrill potato wedges, first parboil them until nearly tender, then drain well and allow to cool completely on a tray. Chargrill them on a hot grill for a few minutes on each side before serving.

SMOKY TOMATO, GARLIC, & LIME SALSA

Serves 4–6

4 vine-ripened tomatoes
2 large green chiles,
    finely sliced
2 garlic cloves, roughly chopped
2 tablespoons lime juice
½ teaspoon sea salt
1 teaspoon superfine sugar
½ cup thinly sliced scallions
1 cup roughly chopped cilantro
    leaves and stalks
organic corn chips, to serve

Thai food was one of my first cuisine crushes, and this recipe is one of the oldest in my repertoire. The Thai version of this salsa would include fish sauce and lime juice. You can just imagine how good that would be, too.

Preheat the grill and hotplate to high.

Put the tomatoes on the grill and cook, turning often, so the skin blisters and blackens. Remove from the heat and leave until cool enough to handle.

Cut out and discard the core of each tomato. Cut the tomatoes in half and gently squeeze out some of the liquid and seeds.

Put the tomatoes, including any bits of burnt skin, in a food processor with the chile and garlic. Blitz until finely chopped, then spoon into a bowl. Stir in the lime juice, salt, sugar, scallion, and cilantro. Check the taste and add more salt if needed.

Loosely wrap the corn chips in foil. Sit the foil parcel on the grill hotplate for a couple of minutes to heat through.

Serve the dip with the warm corn chips on the side.

ARABIAN SPICE MIX

Makes about ½ cup

This is my simplified version of za'atar, a Middle Eastern spice blend. Okay, so the spice mix isn't actually cooked on the grill, but it's such a fabulous accompaniment to grilled foods that I just had to include it. It's particularly delicious sprinkled over chargrilled bread and sliced vine-ripened tomatoes.

2 tablespoons sesame seeds
2 tablespoons dried thyme
2 tablespoons somagh
   (see Notes)
1 teaspoon sea salt
grilled flatbreads, to serve
extra virgin olive oil, to serve

Put the sesame seeds in a small dry frying pan over medium heat. Cook, shaking the pan regularly, until evenly golden. Tip into a bowl and allow to cool.

Put the sesame seeds, thyme, somagh, and salt in a spice mill and process into a rough powder, or grind to a rough powder using a mortar and pestle.

Serve sprinkled on grilled flatbreads dipped in olive oil.

NOTES: Store any unused spice mix in an airtight container in a cool, dark place. It will keep for several months, but is best used within a few weeks for maximum flavor.

Somagh or sumac is a spice ground from a purple berry, widely used in Middle Eastern cuisine. It has a pleasantly astringent lemony flavor and is available from specialty grocers and spice shops.

GREEN TOMATO & CAPER BERRY SALSA

Serves 6–8

4 green tomatoes, cores
    removed, flesh finely diced
½ cup caper berries, chopped
1 red onion, finely diced
¼ cup white vinegar
½ teaspoon sea salt
½ teaspoon superfine sugar
½ cup finely chopped cilantro
    leaves and stalks
½ cup finely chopped mint
grilled haloumi, to serve

This salsa, or sauce, is great spooned over grilled haloumi, tofu, or firm mozzarella cheese. Try tumbling corn chips onto a serving plate and simply topping them with this salsa and some light sour cream. Very nice.

Combine all the ingredients in a serving bowl. Cover and set aside for 30 minutes for the flavors to develop.
    Serve at room temperature.

NOTE: The salsa will keep in an airtight container in the fridge for 2–3 days.

20

VEGETARIAN BARBECUE

JALAPEÑO JAM

Serves 8-10

If chile is your thing, this jam is for you. Spread it over chargrilled bread and spoon over some cottage cheese to cool the heat, or smear it over grilled corn cobs and squeeze some lime juice over to tang it all up a bit. Try sandwiching a layer of the jam and some shredded feta cheese between two soft burritos and cook on the grill hotplate until golden and crisp. Or just keep it in the fridge and put it on anything you like.

1 lb 2 oz green chiles (about 24)
2 garlic cloves
9½ oz jar sliced jalapeño chiles, in vinegar
½ teaspoon sea salt
1 cup sugar
chargrilled bread, to serve
chargrilled vegetables, to serve

Preheat the grill and hotplate to high.

Leave the ends of the chiles intact and scatter the chiles over the hotplate and grill. Cook for 10–15 minutes, using metal tongs to frequently turn the chiles, removing them from the grill as they start to blister and char.

When cool enough to handle, peel off as much of the charred skin as possible. (Leaving some burnt bits is fine as they will add to the final flavor of the jam.)

Pull off and discard the chile stems. Roughly chop the chiles, then place in a food processor with the garlic. Add the whole jar of jalapeños, including the liquid, and blitz until finely chopped.

Tip the paste into a saucepan and stir in the salt and sugar. Bring to the boil, then reduce the heat to a low simmer and cook for 30 minutes, stirring occasionally, until the mixture is thick and sticky-looking. You can test if the jam is ready by placing a spoonful on a cold plate. Run your finger through the middle of the jam — if the mixture stays where it is, the jam is ready.

Serve with chargrilled bread and vegetables.

NOTE: The jam will keep in an airtight container in the fridge for up to 10 days.

23

**DIPS
& BITS**

MUHAMMARA

Serves 6-8

3 large red bell peppers
¼ cup walnuts
1 teaspoon ground cumin
½ teaspoon cayenne pepper
2 tablespoons pomegranate
   molasses
2 tablespoons lemon juice

There are many versions of this dip in Syria, although the combination of roasted red bell peppers, walnuts, and pomegranate molasses can be found in other parts of the Middle East, especially Turkey and Lebanon. Traditionally this dip contains breadcrumbs. I have not included them here, so this version is coeliac friendly.

Preheat the grill to high.

Cook the bell peppers on the grill for 10–15 minutes, turning often, until the skins are blistered and blackened all over. Remove from the grill and allow to cool.

When cool enough to handle, peel and discard the skins. Cut the bell peppers in half, then scoop out and discard the seeds.

Roughly chop the bell pepper flesh and place in a food processor with the remaining ingredients. Process to a smooth, thick mixture.

Spoon into a serving dish and serve.

NOTE: This dip will keep in an airtight container in the fridge for about 1 week.

**VEGETARIAN
BARBECUE**

"BARBIE" GHANOUSH

This one is made for the grill. Actually, I don't believe you can achieve the same flavor without cooking the eggplant over a naked flame. The smokiness of the charred skin somehow gets into the flesh of the eggplant with really very little cooking time.

2 large eggplants
2 teaspoons sea salt
¼ cup lemon juice
3 garlic cloves, crushed
2 tablespoons extra virgin olive oil, plus extra for drizzling
chargrilled Middle Eastern flatbread, to serve

Preheat the grill to high.

Prick each eggplant several times with a fork. Cook them on the grill for 10–15 minutes, turning often, until collapsed and tender. Remove from the grill and allow to cool on a tray.

When cool enough to handle, strip off and discard the skin of each eggplant. Place the flesh in a sieve over a bowl and set aside for 15 minutes to drain.

Put the eggplant flesh in a food processor with the salt, lemon juice, garlic, and olive oil. Whiz to a purée, then pour the mixture into a bowl and drizzle with a little more olive oil.

Serve at room temperature, with chargrilled flatbread.

NOTE: The "barbie" ghanoush will keep in an airtight container in the fridge for 2–3 days.

SPANISH DRESSING

Makes about ¾ cup

///

½ cup Spanish extra virgin
    olive oil
2 tablespoons sherry vinegar
2 tablespoons lemon juice
½ teaspoon sea salt

**I use this dressing to toss through salads, douse over
grilled cheese, and to dunk bread in.**

Place all the ingredients in a jar, seal the lid tightly and shake well.
Store in the fridge for up to 2 weeks; shake well before using.

ROASTED GARLIC CRÈME

Serves 6–8

///

2 garlic bulbs, left whole
    and unpeeled
½ teaspoon sea salt
1 cup rice bran oil
2 egg yolks, at room temperature
1 teaspoon mustard powder
2 tablespoons lemon juice

**Similar to an aïoli, this luscious mayo is fabulous with
grilled vegetables, especially root vegetables.**

Preheat the grill hotplate to medium.
    Cut each garlic bulb in half horizontally through the middle. Sit
each garlic half, cut side up, on a small sheet of foil. Sprinkle with
the salt and drizzle with some of the oil. Loosely wrap each garlic
half in the foil and sit them on the hotplate. Cook for 30 minutes,
turning often with tongs, until the garlic is very soft.
    Remove from the heat and allow the garlic to cool in the foil.
Squeeze the softened garlic flesh out of the skins, directly into the
bowl of a food processor, discarding the skins. Add the egg yolks,
mustard powder, and lemon juice and pulse to combine.
    With the motor running, gradually add the remaining oil in
a thin, steady stream and process until the mixture is emulsified
and looks like thick custard. Add about ¼ cup warm water and
blend until smooth and creamy.
    Serve warm, or cover and keep in the fridge for up to 3 days.

28

**VEGETARIAN
BARBEQUE**

NO FRILLS HOLLANDAISE

No frills because you don't need a double boiler, and no frills because it saves on washing up. Dip in some potato wedges, hot off the grill.

2 egg yolks, at room temperature
½ teaspoon sea salt
¼ cup rice bran oil
4½ oz unsalted/sweet butter
2 tablespoons tarragon vinegar

Put the egg yolks and salt in a food processor and whiz to combine. With the motor running, slowly add the oil in a thin, steady stream and process until the mixture thickens slightly.

Put the butter in a small saucepan and cook over medium heat until bubbling hot, but not burnt. Pour the butter into a pitcher.

With the motor running, slowly pour the hot butter into the egg mixture. Add the vinegar and process until the mixture resembles custard.

Serve the hollandaise warm, or pour into an airtight container and keep in the fridge for up to 3 days.

TZATZIKI

Serves 8

This dip is best enjoyed as soon as it is made. It's great with falafel — either dip the falafel straight in, or smear the tzatziki over flatbread before wrapping up some lightly mashed falafel, fresh tomato, and crisp lettuce.

1½ cups Greek-style yogurt
2 garlic cloves, crushed
1 teaspoon ground cumin
½ teaspoon sea salt
1 small cucumber, coarsely
  shredded

Combine the yogurt, garlic, cumin, and salt in a bowl. Stir the cucumber through just before serving.

GRILLED SWEETCORN & SOUR CREAM DIP

Serves 6–8

4 whole fresh corn cobs,
    preferably unpeeled
1 tablespoon rice bran oil
2 teaspoons dijon mustard
1 red onion, sliced into thick
rings
½ cup finely chopped cilantro
    leaves and stalks, plus extra
    leaves to garnish
3 tablespoons chopped flat-leaf
    parsley
1 tablespoon white wine vinegar
½ teaspoon hot pepper sauce,
    plus extra for drizzling
1 teaspoon sea salt
1½ cups sour cream
warm flatbread, to serve

I have a café in the grounds of an art gallery. We made this dip to be photographed and afterwards I served it up to the staff at the gallery. Wow, what a positive response this one received. I served the dip with a crusty baked baguette and it was devoured in no time.

Preheat the grill to high.

Peel the corn and discard the husks. Brush the corn with the oil and the mustard. Brush the onion rings on both sides with the oil. Grill the corn and onion for 10–12 minutes, or until golden, turning often. Remove from the grill and allow to cool.

Cut the kernels from the cobs and place in a food processor. Roughly chop the onions and add them with the cilantro, parsley, vinegar, pepper sauce, and salt. Whiz until well combined but not too finely chopped — you want some texture in the dip.

Just before serving, combine the corn mixture and the sour cream in a bowl. Drizzle with extra pepper sauce, garnish with extra cilantro and serve with warm flatbread.

30

VEGETARIAN BARBECUE

SMALL PLATES

This is sociable food. This is tasty food, packed with lots of flavor. And that is the key to any cocktail food, finger food or plattered food. The grill can be used to entertain on any level.

Whatever you call it, this is flavorful food enjoyed in a few quick bites, leaving you wanting more. So, for maximum taste I use lots of seasoning in the form of spices. Fragrant and aromatic spices that excite the palate. And let's not forget lots of citrus, chile, and herbs.

You may not think that "cheese" and "barbecue" go together. But some cheeses are made to grill — like the salty, hard haloumi, smoked mozzarella, Indian paneer, or Maltese gbejna. And these cheeses hold their own with strong flavors. They can be cubed and skewered, or bundled up in vine leaves.

The following small plates are a good way to start the occasion. Serve up several choices and pass them around for a very social grill.

GRILLED LOTUS WITH SPICED JAPANESE SALT

Serves 4

10½ oz fresh lotus root,
  peeled and cut into thin slices
2 tablespoons tamari (Japanese
  soy sauce)
1 teaspoon sesame oil
lemon wedges, to serve

SPICED JAPANESE SALT
½ teaspoon white sesame seeds
½ teaspoon black sesame seeds
2 teaspoons sea salt
¼ teaspoon cayenne pepper
2 tablespoons finely chopped
  nori (dried seaweed)

I would not expect you to find fresh lotus root. Although, if you do, please use it. Frozen lotus root is sold in Asian supermarkets and is easier to slice than fresh lotus root, and for best results in this recipe, it does need to be sliced thinly. If you are new to the flavor of lotus root, I can best describe it as nutty and savory — very nicely complemented by the spiced Japanese salt.

Put the lotus slices in a flat dish with the soy sauce and sesame oil and turn to coat. Cover and refrigerate for 3–6 hours, turning often.

To make the spiced Japanese salt, put all the sesame seeds and the salt in a small frying pan. Cook over high heat, shaking the pan, until the mixture just starts to smoke and the white sesame seeds and salt begin to lightly color — be careful not to burn the seeds or they will become bitter.

Remove from the heat and allow to cool. Stir in the cayenne pepper and nori and transfer to an airtight container.

Preheat the grill to high.

Cook the lotus for 2–3 minutes on each side, or until golden.

Serve sprinkled with the spiced salt, with lemon wedges on the side for squeezing over.

NOTE: Any unused spiced salt will keep in an airtight jar in a cool, dark place for up to 1 month. It is also delicious as a seasoning sprinkled over plain boiled rice, tofu, boiled eggs, and avocado.

**VEGETARIAN
BARBECUE**

GRILLED CORN WITH JALAPEÑO, LIME, & PARMESAN BUTTER

Serves 4

This recipe could easily be in the "Sides & Salads" chapter. But whenever I have eaten this I haven't wanted to share it, so it subsequently became my very own small plate.

It might sound odd, but the Parmesan really does work a treat with the bite and tang of the other ingredients. It actually complements them. Because there are so few ingredients here, quality is the key: Good butter, good cheese.

Put all the ingredients for the jalapeño, lime, and Parmesan butter in a food processor and whiz until smooth. Scrape into a bowl, then cover and refrigerate until needed.

Preheat the grill to high. Cut the jalapeño, lime, and Parmesan butter into small pieces and leave at room temperature.

Cook the corn on the hotplate for 10–12 minutes, turning often, until the kernels are dark and caramelized.

Using metal tongs, put the hot corn cobs in a bowl. Add the butter and toss the corn around so it melts the butter.

Tumble the corn cobs onto a serving plate and pour over any melted butter remaining in the bowl. Garnish with cilantro and serve with lime cheeks.

NOTE: You can make the jalapeño, lime, and Parmesan butter up to a week ahead, or wrap it thoroughly and freeze for up to 1 month.

4 corn cobs, each cut into
   3 smaller rounds
cilantro sprigs, to garnish
lime cheeks, to serve

JALAPEÑO, LIME &
PARMESAN BUTTER
4½ oz unsalted/sweet butter,
   softened to room temperature
2 tablespoons pickled jalapeño
   chiles, well drained
   and chopped
1 tablespoon lime juice
¼ cup finely shredded Parmesan
   cheese

37

SMALL PLATES

BLACKENED PANEER SKEWERS

Serves 4

14 oz block paneer
lemon wedges, to serve

BLACKENED SEASONING
¼ cup rice bran oil
2 teaspoons dried thyme
2 teaspoons dried oregano
2 teaspoons hot smoked
    Spanish paprika
1 teaspoon cayenne pepper
1 teaspoon sea salt

FRESH TOMATO RELISH
2 plum tomatoes, finely diced
1 small red onion, finely diced
2 teaspoons soft brown sugar
2 tablespoons lime juice
½ teaspoon celery seeds
¼ teaspoon nigella seeds
    (see Note)

Paneer is an Indian "cheese," though not what Westerners would call cheese. It is a fresh cheese and does not use a setting agent. Have you ever left fresh ricotta in the fridge for several days? It becomes very firm, just like paneer — which, by the way, is so good in curries too.

Combine the blackened seasoning ingredients in a bowl, then pour the mixture onto a flat plate.

Cut the paneer into eight rectangles, about ⅝ inch wide and 2½ inches long — like fat chips. Roll each piece in the blackened seasoning mixture to coat all over. Cover and marinate in the refrigerator for several hours.

Soak eight bamboo skewers in cold water for 30 minutes.

Meanwhile, combine all the tomato relish ingredients in a bowl and set aside for the flavors to develop.

Preheat the grill to high. Thread a bamboo skewer through each piece of paneer. Cook the skewers, turning every couple of minutes, for 8–10 minutes, or until dark and aromatic. Serve immediately, with the tomato relish and lemon wedges.

NOTE: Nigella seeds look like little black sesame seeds, but have a peppery, smoky flavor. They are widely used throughout India, Egypt, and the Middle East. You'll find them in spice shops and gourmet food stores.

38

GRILLED MOZZARELLA WITH TOMATO, HONEY, & CINNAMON JAM

Serves 4

Imagine this... I go to an Italian restaurant in the middle of nowhere, run by women from Rome. A starter dish of simply grilled smoked mozzarella (but, just quietly, the cheese works just as well unsmoked) appears. It is utterly delicious. This is my version, grill style.

Cut the mozzarella into eight slices, about ½ inch thick. Keep the cheese cold in the fridge until you are ready to cook it.

To make the jam, heat the oil in a small saucepan over high heat. Add the onion and cook for 2–3 minutes, or until softened and starting to turn golden. Add the sugar and stir for a minute or so. The sugar will crystallize and the onion will deepen in color.

Carefully add the tomato — it will bubble on contact with the hot sugar. Stir in the cinnamon, reduce the heat to medium and simmer for 5 minutes, stirring often, until the tomato deepens in color. Stir in the honey and cook for a further 10 minutes, stirring often so the mixture doesn't stick to the pan.

Preheat the grill or hotplate to high and lightly brush with oil. Lay the mozzarella slices on the hotplate and cook for 1 minute, or until the edges just start to melt. Quickly turn the slices over and cook for another minute.

Serve hot, with a good dollop of jam and a sprinkling of parsley.

NOTE: Choose the firmest brand of mozzarella available. Fresh mozzarella cannot be cooked this way.

You can also serve each slice of mozzarella on a treviso or radicchio leaf and sprinkle the dolloped jam with sesame seeds.

1 lb 2 oz smoked mozzarella (see Note)
rice bran oil, for brushing
finely chopped parsley, to garnish

TOMATO, HONEY, & CINNAMON JAM
1 tablespoon rice bran oil
1 small red onion, cut in half lengthways, then cut into thin wedges
1 tablespoon superfine sugar
14 oz can chopped tomatoes
½ teaspoon ground cinnamon
2 tablespoons honey

41

SMALL PLATES

HALOUMI, MINT, & PRESERVED LEMON CIGARS

Serves 4–6

6 filo pastry sheets, each
    measuring 17½ x 11¼ inches
7 oz block haloumi cheese
2 tablespoons finely chopped
    mint leaves
2 tablespoons olive oil
12 thin strips of preserved
    lemon rind
sea salt, for sprinkling
lemon wedges, to serve

I love filo pastry. I use it to top, to wrap, to stuff, and to roll, savory or sweet. It's cheap, and you might be surprised to learn that it cooks very well on a hotplate. Enter the grill. Need I say more.

Lay the filo sheets on top of each other. Cut the stack in half lengthways, then cut across in half to give 24 smaller rectangles of pastry. Lay the rectangles on top of each other and cover with a damp cloth.

Cut the haloumi into 12 thin fingers. Combine the mint and olive oil in a bowl.

Lay two filo rectangles on top of each other and brush with some of the oil from the bowl. Put a piece of haloumi on the short end of the pastry, top with a strip of preserved lemon, then fold the sides of the filo over the haloumi and roll up into a cigar shape. Repeat to make 12 cigars.

Preheat the grill hotplate to medium.

Cook the cigars on the hotplate for 4–5 minutes, turning often, until the pastry is golden and charred. Sprinkle with a little sea salt and serve hot, with lemon wedges on the side.

42

**VEGETARIAN
BARBECUE**

CHICKPEA & SQUASH PAKORA

Serves 4–6

Best put, a pakora is a fried snack — although we are grilling them, not frying them here. These fritters are delicious, made even more so by their simplicity.

Bring a large saucepan of water to a boil. Add the chickpeas and squash and cook for 15 minutes, or until the squash is tender. Drain well, then tip the chickpeas and squash into a bowl.

Use a potato masher to mash the chickpeas and squash into a lumpy mixture. Sir in the peas, chile, scallions, besan, cumin, ground coriander, cilantro, lemon juice, and salt. Cover and refrigerate until chilled.

Divide the mixture into eight even portions. Using wet hands, form the portions into disks or patties. Place on a tray lined with parchment paper and refrigerate until ready to cook.

Preheat the grill hotplate to medium–high and brush with oil. Lightly dust the fritters with extra besan and place them on the hotplate. Cook for 3–4 minutes on each side, or until golden.

Serve warm, garnished with cilantro leaves, lettuce, lemon wedges, and yogurt on the side.

NOTE: These fritters can be made a day in advance. Cover with plastic wrap and refrigerate until you're ready to cook them.

10½ oz canned chickpeas, drained
1 lb 2 oz piece of firm squash, peeled, seeded and roughly chopped, to yield about 10½ oz flesh
1 cup frozen peas
1 large green chile, thinly sliced on an angle
2 scallions, thinly sliced on an angle
½ cup besan (chickpea flour) plus extra for dusting
1 teaspoon cumin seeds
1 teaspoon ground coriander
3 tablespoons finely chopped cilantro leaves and stalks, plus extra leaves to garnish
1 tablespoon lemon juice
½ teaspoon sea salt
rice bran oil, for brushing
iceberg lettuce leaves, to serve
lemon wedges, to serve
plain yogurt, to serve

45

EXOTIC EGGPLANT SKEWERS WITH THAI HERB SALAD

Serves 8

12 round Thai green eggplants
¼ cup kecap manis
1 tablespoon rice bran oil

THAI HERB SALAD
2 cups roughly chopped
    cilantro leaves and stalks
2 cups Thai basil leaves
2 cups mint leaves
½ cup finely sliced red Asian
    shallots
2 long red chiles, finely sliced
    on an angle

DRESSING
1 tablespoon Maggi seasoning
1 tablespoon lemon juice
2 teaspoons sesame oil
1 teaspoon superfine sugar

I am a fan of the Thai eggplant varieties. The small pea or round apple eggplants have a crunchy bitterness that works well on the grill. But if they're not your thing, use your favorite eggplant instead, cut into large chunks. It will work just as nicely.

Cut each eggplant in half. Place in a bowl with the kecap manis and oil, tossing to coat well. Cover and set aside for 3 hours for the flavors to penetrate.

Soak eight long bamboo skewers in cold water for 30 minutes.

Meanwhile, combine the Thai herb salad ingredients in a bowl and set aside. Combine the dressing ingredients in a small bowl, stir to dissolve the sugar, then set aside also.

Preheat the grill to high.

Thread the eggplant onto the skewers. Place on the grill and cook, turning often, for 8–10 minutes, or until the eggplant is very tender. Arrange the skewers and salad on a serving platter.

Stir the dressing again, drizzle it over the salad and eggplant and serve.

46

VEGETARIAN BARBECUE

INDIAN BREAD WITH TRUCK-STOP POTATOES

Serves 6–8

2 large boiling potatoes,
(about 1 lb 5 oz), cut into
quarters
1 teaspoon sea salt
½ teaspoon dried mango powder
(see Note)
½ teaspoon chile powder
1 teaspoon toasted cumin seeds
1 teaspoon garam masala
1 cup finely chopped cilantro
leaves and stalks
1 large green chile, finely
chopped
8 ready-made, yeast-free naan
roti
Indian fruit chutney or pickle,
to serve

In India, local roadside restaurants, usually located at highway truck-stops, are called dhabas. I guess the equivalent in the West would be roadside diners. Give me the food in a dhaba any time, which is typically home-made and heavily spiced — just how I like it. The bread in a dhaba would be yeasted and stuffed with the potatoes.

I have adapted this recipe to use ready-made, yeast-free flatbread. Quick, easy, and extremely tasty.

Peel the potatoes and place in a saucepan. Add enough cold water to just cover them and place over high heat. When the water boils, cover the pan and turn the heat off. Leave for 20 minutes, or until the potatoes are tender but not falling apart. (This is also a great way to cook potatoes for a potato salad — they always have the perfect firmness!)

Drain the potatoes and allow to cool to room temperature. When cool enough to handle, coarsely shred the potatoes into a bowl. Add the salt, spices, cilantro, and chile and stir until just combined.

Preheat the grill hotplate to medium.

Spread half the potato mixture over a piece of naan roti and lay another on top. Press down gently to join the two together. Repeat to make another three potato breads.

Cook the breads on the hotplate until just golden on both sides. Cut into thick wedges and serve warm, with your favorite Indian chutney or pickle.

NOTE: Also called amchur or amchoor, dried mango powder is made from ground dried green mangoes and is used in northern Indian cookery to add a tangy, sour, fruit flavor to dishes. You'll find it in Indian grocery stores and good spice shops.

48

**VEGETARIAN
BARBECUE**

SMOKED TOFU, CHILE, & VEGETABLE CABBAGE ROLLS

Serves 4

Cabbage leaves are used in so many cuisines, especially throughout Asia. And anything rolled in them is good — it means you can make them in advance, refrigerate them, then cook them up at a minute's notice.

Bring a large saucepan of water to the boil. Add the cabbage leaves, turn the heat off and set aside for 2 minutes — the leaves will be tender but bright green.

Drain well and rinse under cold water until completely cool. Drain, then trim any thick ends off the cabbage leaves. Lay the leaves on a clean cloth on a work surface and leave to dry.

To make the filling, combine the tofu, sprouts, carrot, ginger, chile, and cilantro in a bowl. Combine the tamari, sesame oil, vinegar, sugar, and cornstarch in another bowl, then pour the mixture over the vegetables. Season to taste with freshly ground black pepper and stir to combine.

To assemble, place about ½ cup of the filling on the broad end of one cabbage leaf. Fold the end over the filling, then fold the sides in, rolling to enclose the filling, and finishing at the stem of the leaf. Don't wrap too tightly, and don't worry if some of the filling sticks out the sides. Repeat with the remaining filling and leaves to make eight rolls.

Tear off eight pieces of foil, large enough to fully wrap up the cabbage rolls, and lay them on a flat surface. Brush the top of each piece of foil with oil. Roll each of the cabbage rolls up in a sheet of foil, twisting the ends to seal.

Preheat a grill hotplate to medium. Sit the cabbage rolls on the hotplate and cook for 10 minutes, turning every few minutes.

Serve the rolls on a platter, to be unwrapped at the table.

8 large napa cabbage
(wong bok) leaves
grape seed oil, for brushing

FILLING
3½ oz smoked tofu, roughly
shredded
1 cup bean sprouts
1 cup shredded carrot
1 teaspoon finely shredded fresh
ginger
1 small red chile, finely sliced
½ cup finely chopped cilantro
leaves and stalks
2 tablespoons tamari (Japanese
soy sauce)
1 teaspoon sesame oil
1 tablespoon rice vinegar
½ teaspoon sugar
1 teaspoon cornstarch

HALOUMI WITH PICKLED CHILE & CAULIFLOWER SALSA

I am thinking I like the word salsa, which really means sauce: It evokes such a sense of freshness and simplicity of flavor. And here the star player is cauliflower, which is often overlooked, yet lends itself to all styles of cooking — baking, frying, boiling. Just serve it with something cheesy and it shines.

To make the salsa, heat the olive oil in large frying pan over high heat. Add the cauliflower and stir-fry for 4–5 minutes, or until golden and tender.

Stir the garlic and onion through and cook for just a minute, then remove from the heat and allow to cool.

Stir in the vinegar, chiles, and herbs. Set aside while cooking the haloumi, to allow the flavors to develop.

Preheat the grill to high.

Brush the haloumi with the rice bran oil. Spread the slices on the grill and cook for 2–3 minutes on each side, or until golden grill marks appear.

Layer the haloumi and salsa on a serving plate. Serve warm.

14 oz haloumi, cut into
    slices ¼ inch thick
1 tablespoon rice bran oil

PICKLED CHILE &
CAULIFLOWER SALSA
1 tablespoon light olive oil
2 cups small cauliflower florets
1 garlic clove, finely chopped
1 red onion, chopped
2 tablespoons sherry vinegar
½ cup finely sliced pickled
    red chiles
3 tablespoons finely shredded
    mint leaves
3 tablespoons finely chopped
    flat-leaf parsley

MALTESE CHEESE WITH OLIVE, PARSLEY, & PRESERVED LEMON SALAD

Serves 6

12 large vine leaves in brine, drained
6 individual Maltese cheeses, about 2¾ oz each
2 tablespoons olive oil

OLIVE, PARSLEY, & PRESERVED LEMON SALAD
½ cup kalamata olives, pitted and chopped
1 cup roughly chopped flat-leaf parsley
1 tablespoon finely chopped preserved lemon rind
2 spring scallions, thinly sliced
1 garlic clove, crushed
¼ cup olive oil
2 tablespoons lemon juice

At my local market, new ingredients come along every now and then and take my fancy. Gbejna, a cheese from Malta, is here to stay. It's not a precious cheese and it likes going with other strong flavors. You could instead use a firm ricotta, which will also hold its own with the lovely, intense flavors of olive and preserved lemon.

Soak the vine leaves in cold water for 30 minutes. Drain well and pat dry.

Lay two vine leaves on a work surface so they slightly overlap. Sit one of the cheeses on one end of the leaves. Drizzle with some of the olive oil, then wrap the cheese up in the vine leaves.

Repeat with the remaining vine leaves, cheese, and oil to make six parcels.

Combine all the salad ingredients in a bowl. Set aside while grilling the cheese.

Preheat the grill to high. Sit the vine leaf parcels on the grill and cook, without turning, for 4–5 minutes, or until the cheese has heated through.

To serve, unwrap the cheeses and spoon the salad on top.

VEGETARIAN BARBECUE

CRISP VEGETABLE & HERB RICE PAPER ROLLS

Makes 12 rolls

I sometimes ask myself why it took me so long to realize the enjoyment of a rice paper roll. These are so yummy; fresh, fragrant, and healthy. Well, they feel healthy. The rice paper itself is like thick cellophane, and is often served fresh after a brief soaking in cold water, rendering the sheets tender enough to fold around favored ingredients. But the rolls can also be deep-fried, pan-fried, or even cooked on a grill!

Soak the noodles in warm water for 10 minutes, or until softened. Drain well in a colander. Use kitchen scissors to roughly chop the noodles into shorter lengths so they are easier to work with.

Combine the noodles in a bowl with the scallions, herbs, garlic chives, carrots, bean sprouts, and zucchini.

Combine the dipping sauce ingredients in a bowl and set aside.

Put some cold water in a flat dish that is wider than the rice paper rolls. Lay a clean cloth on a work surface.

Working one at a time, soak a rice paper sheet in the water for 2 minutes, until the rice paper is white and very soft. Lay the softened sheet flat on the cloth.

Take 3 tablespoons of the filling mixture and form a mound in the middle of the rice paper. Fold the sides over, then roll up to enclose the filling, to make a parcel. Repeat to make 12 rolls.

Preheat the grill hotplate to high and brush with a little rice bran oil. Sit the rolls on the hotplate and cook, turning often, for 4–5 minutes, or until golden all over.

Serve immediately, with the dipping sauce on the side.

NOTE: The dipping sauce can be made ahead and will keep for some days in the fridge in an airtight container.

1¾ oz rice vermicelli noodles
1 cup finely shredded scallions
1 cup chopped cilantro leaves and stalks
1 cup chopped mint leaves
3 tablespoons finely chopped garlic chives
1 cup shredded carrot
1 cup bean sprouts
1 cup shredded zucchini
12 large round rice paper sheets, about 8¼ inches in diameter
rice bran oil, for brushing

DIPPING SAUCE
1 cup hoisin sauce
¼ cup orange juice
½ teaspoon sesame oil

57

SMALL PLATES

KAFFIR LIME LEAF & LEMONGRASS TOFU

Serves 2

2 lemongrass stems, pale part
   only, chopped
2 garlic cloves, chopped
2 kaffir lime leaves, thinly sliced
1 tablespoon finely shredded
   fresh ginger
1 tablespoon Maggi seasoning
2 tablespoons vegetable oil
1 teaspoon superfine sugar
10½ oz block firm tofu
kecap manis, to serve
cilantro sprigs, to garnish

I can totally understand if you don't enjoy tofu, as it is often cooked really badly. I mean, if you cooked a beef filet for 20 minutes on each side you probably wouldn't like that either.

Tofu is about texture. It is a chameleon of sorts and takes on the flavors it is cooked with. So when cooked well — and by this I generally mean simply and quickly — and used with other flavors, you will understand why tofu is no longer only enjoyed by vegetarians.

If you can't get your hands on kecap manis, soy sauce with a little brown sugar will do the job nicely.

Put the lemongrass, garlic, lime leaves, ginger, seasoning, oil, and sugar in a food processor and blend to make a chunky sauce.

Transfer the sauce to a bowl and add the tofu. Gently turn the tofu so it is evenly covered in the mixture. Cover and set aside at room temperature for a couple of hours.

Preheat the grill hotplate to medium. Lay a sheet of parchment paper on the hotplate. Sit the tofu on the parchment paper, scraping any sauce from the bowl over the tofu. Cook for 4–5 minutes.

Using a large metal spatula, turn the tofu over; the lemongrass mixture will have cooked golden and charred in some places. Cook for another 5 minutes.

Cut the tofu into thick slices or cubes and transfer to a serving plate. Drizzle with kecap manis, scatter with cilantro, and serve.

**VEGETARIAN
BARBECUE**

SOY & GINGER GRILLED MUSHROOMS

Serves 4

Try not to use really tiny mushrooms here — or for any grill cooking, for that matter. Little ones are a pain to grill. Big, steaky mushrooms, on the other hand, are easy to cook, have more flesh and are tastier.

Combine the wine, soy sauce, rice flour, sesame oil, and ginger in a large bowl. Add the shiitake and Swiss brown mushrooms and toss to coat them in the marinade. Cover and set aside at room temperature for 3 hours, or refrigerate for 6 hours.

Preheat the grill hotplate to high. Pour the rice bran oil over the hotplate to grease it.

Remove the mushrooms from the marinade and tumble them onto the hotplate. Cook for 10–15 minutes, turning them often, until dark, tender, and aromatic.

Add the oyster mushrooms and cook, turning, for 1–2 minutes, or until just tender. Serve hot, scattered with sliced scallions.

1 cup red wine
1 cup light soy sauce
2 tablespoons rice flour
1 tablespoon sesame oil
1 tablespoon finely shredded
   fresh ginger
6 large shiitake mushrooms
6 large Swiss brown mushrooms
2 tablespoons rice bran oil
6 king oyster mushrooms,
   halved lengthways
3½ oz oyster mushrooms
sliced scallions, to serve

BIG PLATES

Many people assume that vegetarians are small eaters. Please don't. Especially so at a grill, where the vegetarian is often overlooked. And please don't let the vegetarian option be a tofu sausage or a frozen pattie. This is insulting to both the individual and to the many cuisines that have vegetarian cookery embedded in their culinary history.

Quite a few of the recipes in this chapter are simply my grilled versions of some of the most delicious vegetarian dishes you can find: North African chakchouka, Chinese Buddha's delight, Japanese pancakes. Many of these dishes are in fact traditionally cooked on a grill or hotplate. And with a little ingenuity, other dishes that weren't originally intended to be cooked on the grill can be given the grill treatment too. With a few tricks under your belt — such as wrapping food in lotus, vine, or banana leaves, or using skewers — anything is possible.

There may well be times when your grill is about grazing, picking, and dipping. But sometimes we want to eat like a man, or a woman. These recipes will fit the bill.

SWISS CHARD & FETA GÖZLEME

Serves 4

1 tablespoon olive oil, plus
extra for brushing
1 red onion, finely chopped
2 garlic cloves, crushed
6 oz finely shredded Swiss chard
7 oz feta cheese, crumbled
½ cup coarsely shredded
cheddar cheese
¼ teaspoon sweet paprika
4 large Greek pita breads, about
10½ inches across
lemon wedges, to serve

Hot dog and donut stalls have been replaced by gözleme (Turkish pizza) stalls at markets. And this is not a bad thing. I love these "pizzas." It would be very tricky to try your hand at making the dough yourself, but you don't have to, not with so many exotic pre-made breads out there — including some good gluten-free ones too.

Combine the olive oil, onion, garlic, Swiss chard, feta, cheddar, and paprika in a bowl, mixing well.

Spread half the mixture over one pita bread and top with another. Repeat with the remaining pita breads and filling to make a second gözleme.

Preheat the grill hotplate to medium–high. Brush both sides of one gözleme with olive oil. Cook the first gözleme for 3–4 minutes on each side, or until crisp and golden, using a metal spatula to compress it. Cut into wedges and serve immediately, with lots of lemon wedges for squeezing over.

Brush both sides of the second gözleme with olive oil and cook it in the same way, while your guests eat the first.

**VEGETARIAN
BARBECUE**

BUDDHA'S DELIGHT

As the name suggests, there is a link between this dish and Buddha. Buddhist monks are known to be partial to this dish, which traditionally would contain at least ten different types of vegetables. In this version I have kept the vegetable list down to include those that cook easily and quickly on the grill. Feel free to add your favorites, but remember that if you add hard vegetables like carrots they'll need parboiling before making it to the grill.

Preheat the grill and hotplate to high.

Pour some of the oil into a large bowl, add the mushrooms and toss to lightly coat. Cook on the grill for 4–5 minutes on each side, or until tender. Remove to a clean bowl and cover to keep warm.

Add a little more oil to the oiled bowl. Add the corn and leek and toss to lightly coat in the oil. Cook on the hotplate for 2–3 minutes on each side, or until tender, then add to the bowl with the mushrooms and cover to keep warm.

Add the remaining oil to the oiled bowl, then lightly coat the bamboo shoots and beans, then the tofu. Add the bamboo shoots and beans to the hotplate, and the tofu to the grill, and cook for 4–5 minutes, or until the bamboo and beans are just tender but crisp, and the tofu is heated through.

Meanwhile, combine all the soy ginger sauce ingredients in a small saucepan, stirring to make sure the cornstarch has dissolved. Cook over medium heat until the mixture boils and turns from a thin, cloudy sauce to one that is clear and thickened.

Tumble the warm cooked vegetables onto a serving plate and pour the sauce over. Serve warm.

NOTE: Whole bamboo shoots are generally sold packed in cryovac bags, available from Asian grocers.

¼ cup rice bran oil
12 large shiitake mushrooms, stems removed
12 Swiss brown mushrooms, stems removed
14 oz baby corn, halved lengthways
4 baby leeks, white part only, halved lengthways
3½ oz peeled whole bamboo shoots, sliced (see Note)
3½ oz green beans, trimmed
10½ oz firm tofu, cut into slices ½ inch thick

SOY GINGER SAUCE
½ cup vegetable broth
1 tablespoon light soy sauce
1 tablespoon finely shredded fresh ginger
½ teaspoon sugar
1 teaspoon cornstarch

MUSHROOM BULGOLGI

Serves 4

7 oz fresh shiitake mushrooms

7 oz oyster mushrooms

7 oz medium-sized field
   mushrooms

4 pine mushrooms, or 2 large
   king oyster mushrooms,
   thickly sliced

1 teaspoon toasted sesame
   seeds

MARINADE

¼ cup Korean or Japanese
   soy sauce

1 tablespoon sesame oil

1 teaspoon toasted sesame
   seeds

2 scallions, thinly sliced
   on an angle

2 garlic cloves, finely chopped

1 tablespoon finely shredded
   fresh ginger

Okay, so bulgolgi is a popular Korean steak recipe, which translates to something like "fired meat." With this recipe, the flavor comes from the marinade. I love a good steak myself, but why should meat get all the fun?

Combine the marinade ingredients in a bowl.

Cut off and discard any large stems from the mushrooms. Lay the mushrooms in a large, flat dish, pour the marinade over and turn to coat. Cover and refrigerate for 3 hours, or overnight, turning the mushrooms every now and then.

Remove the mushrooms from the fridge 30 minutes before cooking to bring them to room temperature.

Preheat the grill to medium.

Use tongs to shake the excess marinade off the mushrooms, then arrange them on the grill. Cook the mushrooms, turning them often, for 10–15 minutes, or until dark, tender and aromatic.

Serve warm, sprinkled with the sesame seeds.

**VEGETARIAN
BARBECUE**

LIME & TURMERIC TOFU STEAKS WITH FRESH SAMBAL

Serves 4

The real flavor in this recipe comes from the sambal, and as far as flavors go, you won't be left wanting. Sambal is a chile-based condiment used throughout South-East Asia. It is generally cooked, but this is a very raw, very fresh, and very tasty version.

Combine the sambal ingredients in a bowl and stir until the broth powder has dissolved. Cover and set aside for 30 minutes, or refrigerate overnight.

Cut the tofu into four equal portions. Place in a flat dish in a single layer.

Combine the lime juice, grapeseed oil, and turmeric in a bowl and stir until the turmeric has dissolved and the oil is vibrantly colored. Pour the marinade over the tofu and turn to coat all over. Set aside for 30 minutes.

Preheat the grill to high.

Cook the tofu for 2–3 minutes on each side, or until heated through and slightly crusty. Serve warm, with the sambal spooned over and lime cheeks on the side.

1 lb 5 oz firm tofu
¼ cup lime juice
¼ cup grapeseed oil
¼ teaspoon ground turmeric
lime cheeks, to serve

SAMBAL
1 teaspoon vegetable broth/stock
    powder
2 kaffir lime leaves, thinly sliced
2 lemongrass stems, pale part
    only, finely chopped
2 bird pepper chiles, finely
    chopped

3 tablespoons finely chopped
    red Asian shallots
2 garlic cloves, finely chopped

1 tablespoon vegetable oil

1 tablespoon lime juice

71

BIG PLATES

GRILLED SQUASH GNOCCHI WITH GREEN CHILE CREAM

Serves 4

½ butternut squash,
    about 2 lb 4 oz, or
    you can use the top end
    of a larger squash
½ cup fine semolina,
    plus extra for sprinkling
2 tablespoons finely shredded
    Parmesan cheese, plus
    extra to garnish
1 egg, lightly beaten
rice bran oil, for brushing
flat-leaf parsley, to garnish

GREEN CHILE CREAM
1 cup single cream
1 large green chile, split down
    the middle
¼ cup finely shredded Parmesan
    cheese

The idea for this tasty number stems from Roman gnocchi, which is baked and cut into larger pieces than the little "pillow" gnocchi we are familiar with.

Preheat the grill hotplate to medium.

Wrap the squash in two layers of foil. Sit the whole squash on the hotplate. Cook for 1 hour, turning the squash over every 20 minutes, until firm when pierced with a skewer or knife. Remove from the heat and allow the squash to cool in the foil.

Preheat the oven to 350°F/Gas 4.

Unwrap the squash, scoop out the seeds, and discard. Scoop the tender squash flesh into a bowl — you should have about 2–2½ cups. Mash well, then stir in the semolina, Parmesan, and egg until smooth.

Lightly grease a 10 x 3¼ x 2 inch bar pan with oil. Sprinkle a little of the semolina over the base and sides. Spoon the mixture into the loaf pan and bake for 25–30 minutes, or until just set. Remove from the oven, cool to room temperature, then refrigerate until cold.

To make the green chile cream, put the cream and chile in a saucepan. Cook over low heat until the cream simmers, but does not boil up. Now simmer for 10 minutes, or until thickened. Stir the Parmesan through, then pour into a serving pitcher or thermos to keep warm.

Preheat the grill to high. Cut the gnocchi mixture into 12 slices, about ¾ inch thick. Brush each of the cut sides with oil. Cook on the grill for 2–3 minutes on each side, or until golden and heated through — don't be tempted to move the gnocchi early, or they will stick to the grill.

Arrange the gnocchi on a platter. Drizzle with the warm green chile cream and serve scattered with parsley and extra Parmesan.

VEGETARIAN BARBECUE

PANEER & TOMATO SKEWERS

Serves 6

Paneer is a fresh, lightly pressed Indian "cheese," though not really a cheese in the same sense as many of us would think, as it doesn't have a setting agent like rennet. Like haloumi, it grills well. It can be cubed or cut into steaks and cooked until golden.

Soak 12 bamboo skewers in cold water for 30 minutes.

Meanwhile, combine the dressing ingredients in a bowl and set aside for the flavors to infuse.

Preheat the grill hotplate to high. Lightly brush with olive oil.

Alternately thread two pieces of paneer and two cherry tomatoes onto each skewer. Sprinkle with the cumin and fennel seeds.

Lay the skewers on the hotplate and cook for 8–10 minutes, turning often, until the paneer is golden and the tomatoes softened.

Arrange on a serving platter and drizzle with the dressing. Serve warm, with lemon cheeks for squeezing over.

olive oil, for brushing
14 oz paneer, cut into
     1 inch cubes
24 cherry tomatoes
1 teaspoon cumin seeds
1 teaspoon fennel seeds
lemon cheeks, to serve

HERB & CHILE DRESSING
1 large red chile, thinly sliced
     on an angle
¼ cup light olive oil
1 teaspoon sea salt
1 cup roughly chopped cilantro
     leaves
1 cup roughly chopped mint
     leaves
2 tablespoons lemon juice

JAPANESE VEGETABLE & GINGER PANCAKES

Serves 2

½ cup all-purpose flour
1 cup vegetable broth
2 eggs
2 teaspoons finely shredded
fresh ginger
1 cup thinly sliced scallions
5½ oz shiitake mushrooms,
stems discarded, caps thinly
sliced
2 cups finely shredded napa
cabbage (wong bok)
rice bran oil, for brushing
Japanese mayonnaise, to serve
pickled ginger, to serve
nori flakes mixed with toasted
sesame seeds, for sprinkling

These are called okonomiyaki, which translates to "cook your own" or "cook it yourself." Which is what grilling is all about, right?

So tasty and easy to make, they're a really great vegetarian barbecue meal on their own. Many of the recipes here are for sharing, and you could indeed share these pancakes. But I imagine them to be enjoyed like a grilled steak — as a solo barbecue eating experience, with nothing more than a few extra tasty bits on the side.

Put the flour in a bowl. Combine the broth and eggs in another bowl and whisk until well combined. Add the broth mixture to the flour and whisk until smooth. Stir in the ginger, scallions, mushroom, and cabbage.

Preheat the grill hotplate to medium and brush with oil.

Using one level cupful of the mixture for each omelette, measure four level cupfuls onto the grill to make four omelettes, gently patting them down with a spatula into rough circles about 5–6 inches across. Spoon any remaining mixture equally over the omelettes.

Cook for 5 minutes, or until a golden crust starts to form around the edges. Use a large spatula to flip the omelettes over. Cook for another 5 minutes.

Serve warm, with Japanese mayonnaise, pickled ginger, and mixed nori flakes and sesame seeds on the side as condiments.

VEGETARIAN BARBECUE

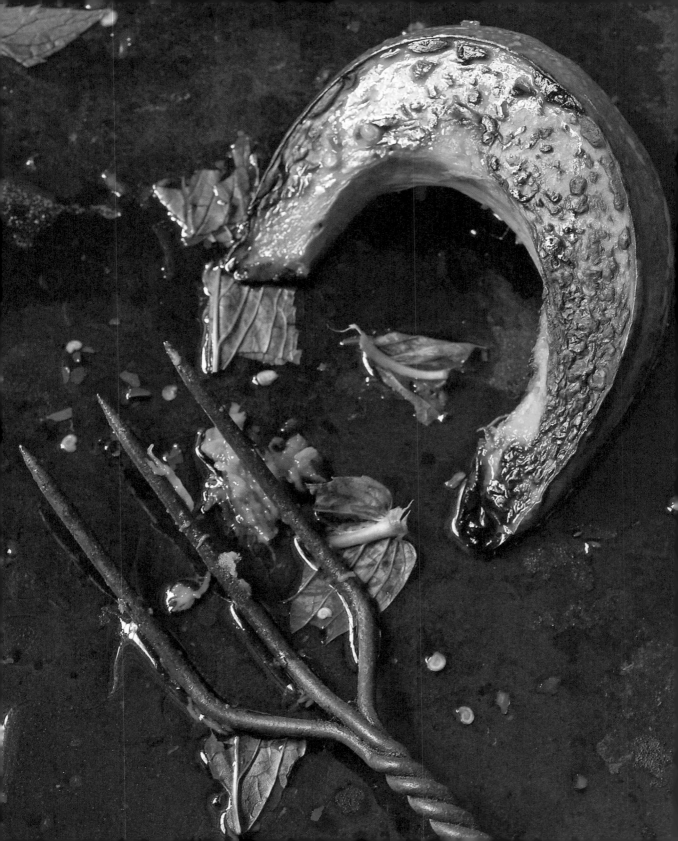

SPANISH EGG POTS

Serves 4

I've been making these Spanish eggs at my café for years now. It is the most simple brunch dish, and very tasty — even easier if you make the tomato mixture a day ahead.

2 tablespoons olive oil
1 red onion, sliced into thin wedges
¼ cup thinly sliced roasted red bell pepper strips
1 lb 12 oz can chopped tomatoes
3 tablespoons finely chopped flat-leaf parsley, plus extra to garnish
4 eggs
extra virgin olive oil, for drizzling
chargrilled bread, to serve

Heat the olive oil in a saucepan over medium heat. Add the onion and cook for 2–3 minutes, or until the onion softens. Add the bell pepper and stir-fry together, then stir the tomato and parsley through. Season to taste with salt and freshly ground black pepper.

Bring to a boil and cook for 8–10 minutes, or until the tomato mixture is thick. (You can cool and refrigerate the mixture at this stage, and reheat just before using, although I prefer to use it straight away.)

Preheat the grill or hotplate to high.

Sit four 1½–2 cup heatproof dishes on the grill to heat up. Spoon about 1 cup of the mixture into each dish and let it get bubbling hot. Use a spoon to make a hollow in the middle of each one, then crack an egg into each dish.

Cover each dish with foil or a small plate and cook for 3–4 minutes, or until the egg whites are firm and the yolks are soft.

Serve hot, with a sprinkling of parsley and a drizzle of extra virgin olive oil, with warm chargrilled bread on the side.

81

BIG PLATES

WHOLE BAKED RICOTTA WITH WARM TOMATO & OLIVE SALSA

Serves 6–8

olive oil, for brushing
2 lb 4 oz fresh ricotta
1 teaspoon sea salt

TOMATO & OLIVE SALSA
¼ cup olive oil
24 small truss cherry tomatoes,
 preferably still on the vine
4 thyme sprigs
2 garlic cloves, finely chopped
⅓ cup sherry vinegar
½ cup small black olives, pitted
 and roughly chopped
⅓ cup small salted capers,
 well rinsed
3 tablespoons finely chopped
 flat-leaf parsley

I have used one of my favorite grilling tricks here: By laying a sheet of parchment paper on the grill or hotplate, you can cook ingredients that might otherwise get stuck. You can also then use the parchment paper to tip the cooked ingredients into a bowl or directly onto a serving plate.

Preheat the grill or hotplate to high.

Tear off a large sheet of foil and place it on a work surface. Lay a similar-sized piece of parchment paper over the foil. Lightly brush the paper with olive oil to grease it.

Tip the ricotta out onto the parchment paper and sprinkle with the salt. Bring the sides of the foil up to enclose the ricotta, pressing the foil over to seal the ricotta inside. Sit the parcel on the grill or hotplate and cook for 10 minutes, or until the ricotta is heated through. Leave wrapped to keep it warm while making the salsa.

To make the salsa, pour 1 tablespoon of the olive oil into a bowl. Add the tomatoes and thyme and toss to lightly coat the tomatoes in the oil. Tear off a sheet of parchment paper and lay it on the hotplate. Tumble the mixture onto the parchment paper and cook for 3–4 minutes, until the tomatoes have softened.

Carefully pick up the parchment paper sheet by the corners and tumble the tomatoes into a bowl. Add the remaining salsa ingredients. Season to taste with sea salt and freshly ground black pepper and stir well to combine.

Spoon the salsa over the warm ricotta and serve.

82

VEGETARIAN BARBECUE

TOFU, TOMATO, & SHIITAKE SKEWERS WITH GINGER & SCALLION DRESSING

Serves 4

You could try using silky, soft tofu here, but it does tend to stick to the hotplate and break up easily. One way to avoid this is to put some parchment paper on the hotplate. I generally prefer soft tofu, but am using the firm variety in this recipe, simply because it looks better when it makes it to the table.

Soak eight bamboo skewers in cold water for 30 minutes.

To make the dressing, put the ginger and scallions in a small heatproof bowl. Heat the oil in a small saucepan over high heat until smoking hot. Pour the hot oil over the ginger and scallions so they sizzle and soften, then stir in the soy sauce and sesame oil. Set aside while preparing the skewers.

Cut the tofu into pieces about the same size as the tomatoes.

Randomly thread some tofu, three tomatoes, and three mushrooms on each skewer. Put the skewers in a flat dish or on a plate. Combine the oil and soy sauce and brush the mixture over the vegetables and tofu.

Preheat a grill hotplate to high. Cook the skewers for 8 minutes, turning every couple of minutes, until golden and tender.

Spoon the dressing over the skewers. Serve scattered with cilantro sprigs.

NOTE: The ginger and scallion dressing can be made a day in advance. Store it in an airtight container in the fridge until needed and bring back to room temperature before using.

10½ oz firm tofu
24 truss cherry tomatoes
24 small shiitake mushrooms
1 tablespoon rice bran oil
2 teaspoons light soy sauce
cilantro sprigs, to garnish

GINGER & SCALLION DRESSING
2 tablespoons julienned
   fresh ginger
1 cup thinly sliced scallions
¼ cup rice bran oil
2 tablespoons light soy sauce
1 teaspoon sesame oil

BIG MUSHROOMS WITH MARINATED FETA

Serves 4

2 thyme sprigs
2 garlic cloves, sliced
2 scallions, finely sliced
   on an angle
½ cup light olive oil
½ teaspoon sea salt
2 tablespoons sherry vinegar
7 oz semi-soft goat's feta cheese
8 large field mushrooms, or
   pine mushrooms if available
1 teaspoon sumac (see Notes
   on page 19)
finely chopped flat-leaf parsley
   (optional), to garnish

I would say the top two vegetables to cook on the grill are eggplant and mushrooms. They lend themselves to all sorts of cooking styles and pair well with many different flavors. I have made my own herb-infused oil here, but if you can get your hands on soft feta marinated in oil with garlic and herbs, then by all means use that. All you'll then have to do is spoon the ready-marinated cheese into the mushroom caps and cook them on your grill. Very nice.

Put the thyme, garlic, and scallion in a heatproof bowl.

Heat the olive oil in a small frying pan over medium heat. When the oil is smoking hot, pour in the scallion mixture, allowing it to sizzle in the oil and release the flavors. Stir in the salt, vinegar, and some freshly ground black pepper to taste.

Cut the feta into small bite-sized cubes and arrange in a flat non-metallic dish. Spoon the scallion mixture over the feta. Cover and marinate in the refrigerator for up to 3 days.

Preheat the grill to high.

Remove the stems from the mushrooms and spoon some pieces of feta and the marinade into the caps. Sit the mushrooms on the grill, then close the grill lid, or cover the mushrooms with a baking tray. Cook for 15 minutes, or until the mushrooms are tender.

Serve warm, sprinkled with the sumac, and parsley if desired.

VEGETARIAN
BARBECUE

FLAVORS-OF-INDIA PIZZA

Serves 4

Have you ever tried freshly made naan bread? It's pretty good, but not an easy thing to whip up at home. Well, not for most of us anyway.

I wouldn't suggest that we only ever cook with ready-made items, but they do have their place. Convenience is one thing, and some of the packet naan breads out there are okay if they are reheated — so using them for a pizza base seems only logical. And tasty.

1 cup puréed tomatoes
½ teaspoon fennel seeds
½ teaspoon ground cumin
½ teaspoon chile flakes
½ teaspoon sea salt
4 naan breads or roti, each about 6 inches long
1 zucchini, very thinly sliced
1 small red bell pepper, thinly sliced
1 small red onion, very thinly sliced
3½ oz paneer cheese, roughly crumbled
cilantro leaves, to garnish
lime pickle, to serve

Preheat the grill to medium.

Combine the puréed tomatoes, fennel, cumin, chile flakes, and salt in a small bowl.

Sit each naan bread on a double-thickness sheet of parchment paper — this will make it easier to lift the pizzas on and off the grill. Spread the tomato mixture over each naan bread. Randomly scatter the zucchini, bell pepper, and onion over the top, then scatter with the paneer.

Put the pizzas on the grill, then close the grill lid if you have one, or cover the pizzas with a baking tray. Cook for 10 minutes. Lift up the pizzas with a metal spatula to see how they are cooking underneath, just like they do with wood-fired pizzas — a toasty golden brown base is what you are looking for.

Scatter with cilantro leaves and serve warm, with lime pickle on the side.

MISO BROWN RICE IN LOTUS LEAVES

Serves 4

2 large dried lotus leaves
(available from Asian
grocers)
1 tablespoon white miso paste
2 tablespoons light soy sauce
1 teaspoon sesame oil
½ teaspoon sea salt
½ teaspoon sugar
2 tablespoons rice bran oil
2 garlic cloves, finely chopped
1 tablespoon finely shredded
fresh ginger
2 scallions, finely chopped
1 cup finely shredded napa
cabbage (wong bok)
1 cup finely shredded pak choy
or choy sum
1 cup long-grain brown rice,
cooked until tender, then drained

What started as a small plate option turned very quickly into a big one: It was so tasty I couldn't stop eating it! I then realized how full I was afterwards — another good sign, given all the good-for-you things in this dish.

The lotus leaves are a yum cha (or dim sum) inspiration, where it is used as a parcel for sticky rice. Here's another great way to use these aromatic leaves.

Dried lotus leaves are usually folded in half; don't unfold them or they will break. Lay them in the kitchen sink and pour over enough boiling water to cover. Leave for 1 hour, so they become tender and turn the color of fresh grape vine leaves. Remove the leaves from the water. Unfold the leaves and cut in half, removing any stem. Trim each half into 12 inch squares and set aside.

Combine the miso, soy sauce, sesame oil, salt, and sugar in a pitcher. Pour in ½ cup boiling water and stir well to make sure all the miso has dissolved.

Heat the rice bran oil in a frying pan or wok over high heat. Add the garlic, ginger, and scallion and stir-fry for a few seconds, or until aromatic but not burning. Add the cabbage and bok choy and stir-fry for 5 minutes, or until well wilted.

Add the rice and the miso mixture. Stir to combine, then bring to the boil. Reduce the heat to medium and cook for 5 minutes, or until almost all the liquid has been absorbed.

Lay the four lotus leaf squares on a work surface. Spoon one-quarter of the rice mixture into the center of each. Roll the leaves up to make firm parcels.

Preheat the grill hotplate to medium.

Sit the parcels on the hotplate, seam side down, and cook for 10 minutes, until the seam side looks dry and blistered. Turn them over and cook for another 5 minutes. Serve warm.

88

**VEGETARIAN
BARBECUE**

ZUCCHINI, EGGPLANT, & HALOUMI SKEWERS

Serves 4

Haloumi is one of those ingredients that seemed to appear from out of nowhere to become one of my favorite things to cook. Here it is cubed and skewered with eggplant and zucchini. You could also slice the haloumi into "steaks" about ½ inch thick, marinate them in a mixture of chile flakes, dried oregano, olive oil, and lemon juice, then cook on the grill until a golden crust forms. Serve with couscous, if desired.

1 lb 2 oz haloumi cheese
2 Japanese eggplants
2 zucchini
2 tablespoons olive oil, plus extra for brushing
2 tablespoons apple cider vinegar
2 teaspoons cumin seeds
1 teaspoon chile flakes
baby arugula leaves, to serve

Soak eight bamboo skewers in cold water for 30 minutes.

Cut the haloumi, eggplant, and zucchini into ¾ inch chunks. Alternately thread two bits of haloumi onto each skewer with some eggplant and zucchini. Lay the skewers on a flat dish.

Mix the olive oil, vinegar, cumin, and chile in a small bowl, then pour the mixture over the skewers. Cover and set aside at room temperature for a couple of hours for the flavors to infuse.

Preheat the grill hotplate to high. Brush with a little olive oil to lightly grease.

Put the skewers on the hotplate, reserving the marinade in the dish, and cook for 2–3 minutes, or until a dark-golden crust has formed on the haloumi.

Use a metal spatula to turn the skewers over, then cook for another 2 minutes.

Scatter lots of arugula on a serving plate and pile the skewers alongside. Drizzle with the reserved marinade and serve.

FRAGRANT FIVE-SPICE VEGETABLE PARCELS

Serves 4

12 medium-sized shiitake
    mushrooms, stems removed
1 small sweet potato, cut into
    rounds ½ inch thick
7 oz peeled daikon, cut
    into 1¼ inch cubes
7 oz firm tofu, cut into
    ¾ inch pieces
2 tablespoons thinly sliced shiso
    leaves (see Note)
¼ cup good-quality soy sauce
1 tablespoon mirin
½ teaspoon sugar
½ teaspoon Chinese five-spice
1 teaspoon sesame oil

Shiitake mushrooms have such a wonderful savory aroma. Dried shiitakes are even more intense and also work well for this recipe. They store well, are inexpensive and easy to use. Just pour over boiling water to cover
and leave to soften for about 30 minutes, then discard the stems and either use the caps whole or chop them up. This dish is great served with steamed brown rice.

Preheat the grill hotplate to high.

    Combine all the ingredients in a large bowl. Tear off a sheet of foil about 12 inches square and place a similar-sized piece of parchment paper over the foil.

    Spoon a quarter of the vegetable mixture in the middle of the parchment paper. Bring the sides of the foil up to enclose the vegetables, sealing the edges together. Repeat to make four parcels.

    Sit the parcels on the hotplate and cook for 12–15 minutes, or until the vegetables are tender and aromatic. Serve hot.

NOTE: Also known as perilla, and related to mint, shiso is a herb with round, serrated, green, or purplish leaves. If you can't get any, use flat-leaf parsley instead.

VEGETARIAN BARBECUE

GADO GADO WITH SATAY SAUCE

Gado gado, literally meaning "mix mix," is one of the first exotic things I remember eating. Up there with lumpia (Indonesian spring rolls), this dish was what we dined on during our Indonesian language class excursions. Traditionally, this recipe would use fresh or uncooked ingredients. This version uses grilled vegetables, topped off with the satay sauce. And, really, is there anything better than a good satay sauce?

2 zucchini, thickly sliced
    on an angle
1 eggplant, thickly sliced
1 red bell pepper,
    cut into thick strips
7 oz green beans or flat beans
2 small red onions, cut into
    thick wedges, keeping
    the roots intact
2 tablespoons rice bran oil
1 cup bean sprouts

SATAY SAUCE
4½ oz raw peanuts
1½ tablespoons vegetable oil
1 garlic clove, chopped
1 small red chile, chopped
1½ tablespoons light brown sugar
14 fl oz coconut milk
1 tablespoon kecap manis

To make the satay sauce, put the peanuts and vegetable oil in a frying pan over medium heat. When the peanuts start to sizzle, cook for another 2–3 minutes, or until golden, then pour into a metal colander set over a heatproof bowl.

Discard the oil and put the hot peanuts in a food processor with the garlic, chile, and sugar. Whiz until a thick paste forms, then scrape the mixture into a saucepan. Stir in the coconut milk and kecap manis and bring to a boil. Reduce the heat to very low and cook for 20 minutes, or until the mixture is very thick.

Preheat the grill and hotplate to high.

Combine the zucchini, eggplant, and bell pepper in a large bowl, and the beans and onion in another bowl. Add the rice bran oil to both bowls and toss the vegetables around so they are all evenly coated in the oil.

Cooking in batches, tumble the zucchini, bell pepper, and eggplant over the grill, and spread the beans and onions over the hotplate (these are best cooked on the hotplate as they will tend to fall through the grill bars). Cook for 10–15 minutes, removing the vegetables as they become golden and tender; some will cook more quickly than others. Put the cooked vegetables in a bowl and cover to keep warm while the rest are being cooked.

Season the vegetables with sea salt and freshly ground black pepper and pile them onto a serving plate. Top with the bean sprouts. Spoon the satay sauce over, or serve it on the side.

NAKED SAMOSAS

Serves 4

4 medium-sized idaho or king
    edward potatoes
2 tablespoons light olive oil,
    plus extra for brushing
½ teaspoon black mustard seeds
1 onion, thinly sliced
1 garlic clove, finely chopped
2 teaspoons finely shredded
    fresh ginger
½ teaspoon cumin seeds
1 teaspoon fennel seeds
½ cup frozen peas, thawed
¼ teaspoon ground turmeric
2 teaspoons sea salt
¼ teaspoon chile powder
½ teaspoon garam masala
½ cup finely chopped cilantro
    leaves and stalks, plus extra
    leaves, to garnish
mango chutney, to serve
plain yogurt, to serve

So called because they have no pastry. These samosas are more like vegetable patties or burgers, with all the tasty flavors of Indian cooking. You could serve them as a take on a vegetable burger — put the samosa on a piece of warm grilled naan bread and top with chutney, yogurt, and cilantro.

Peel and wash the potatoes. Cut each into eight pieces and place in a saucepan. Cover with cold water, bring to a boil and cook for 15 minutes, or until just tender. Drain well, then tip the potatoes out onto a clean chopping board to cool and dry.

Put the potatoes in a large bowl and roughly mash them.

Heat the olive oil in a frying pan over high heat. Add the mustard seeds and cook until the seeds start to pop. Add the onion and cook, stirring, for 4–5 minutes, or until golden. Now add the garlic, ginger, cumin seeds, and fennel seeds and stir-fry for 1 minute, until aromatic. Mix the peas through.

Pour the onion mixture over the potatoes. Add the turmeric, salt, chile powder, garam masala, and cilantro. Stir together using a large spoon, making sure the ingredients are really well combined. Cover and set aside at room temperature for an hour or two for the flavors to develop, or refrigerate until needed.

Using slightly wet hands, divide the mixture into eight equal portions, then form into balls. Gently pat down into disks or patties.

Preheat the grill hotplate to high. Brush with a little olive oil to lightly grease.

Cook the patties on the hotplate for 10 minutes on each side, or until they have a golden crust.

Serve warm, garnished with cilantro leaves, with chutney and yogurt on the side.

**VEGETARIAN
BARBECUE**

FAT POLENTA CHIPS WITH EGGPLANT, TOMATO, & FRESH MOZZARELLA

Serves 4

I've been making these killer polenta chips for years now. The simple trick is using two types of polenta: Fine and coarse. It might seem overly fussy, but try these and you'll probably agree they're the best you've ever eaten.

Line a 10 x 3¼ x 3¼ inch bar pan with plastic wrap.

Bring the broth to a boil in a saucepan over high heat.

Combine the fine and coarse polenta in a bowl. Pour the polenta into the boiling broth, whisking continuously until smooth and well combined. Reduce the heat to low and stir with a wooden spoon for just a minute, until the mixture is completely smooth. Stir in the Parmesan, butter, and caraway seeds.

Scrape the mixture into the loaf pan and smooth the top with the back of a spoon. Chill for several hours, or overnight, until cold.

Turn the polenta out onto a chopping board. Cut the polenta crossways into 12 thick slices.

Preheat the grill to high.

Put the eggplant and onion in a bowl with a splash of rice bran oil. Season with sea salt and freshly ground black pepper and toss to lightly coat. Spread the vegetables on the grill, so they don't overlap, and cook for 8–10 minutes, turning often, until golden and tender.

Transfer the vegetables to a bowl, add the parsley and chile, and toss to combine. Cover and set aside while cooking the polenta.

Brush the polenta with some oil and cook on the grill for 3–4 minutes on each side, or until grill marks are well formed.

Arrange layers of the polenta, eggplant, and tomato on a serving platter. Roughly tear the mozzarella and scatter over the top. Drizzle with olive oil, garnish with basil leaves, and serve.

3½ cups vegetable broth
4½ oz fine quick-cooking polenta
4½ oz coarse quick-cooking polenta
½ cup finely shredded Parmesan cheese
1 oz unsalted/sweet butter, chopped
½ teaspoon caraway seeds
1 small eggplant, sliced into thick rounds
1 red onion, sliced into thick rounds
rice bran oil, for coating
3 tablespoons roughly chopped flat-leaf parsley
1 large red chile, finely chopped
2 heirloom tomatoes, sliced
extra virgin olive oil, for drizzling
9 oz buffalo mozzarella cheese
basil leaves, to garnish

BIG PLATES

CHAKCHOUKA

Serves 4

¼ cup rice bran oil
6 ripe tomatoes, cut in half
1 small yellow bell pepper,
    cut into strips
1 small green bell pepper,
    cut into strips
1 small red bell pepper,
    cut into strips
1 red onion, cut into rings
1 large red chile, finely chopped
1 teaspoon ground cumin
1 teaspoon sweet paprika
1 teaspoon sea salt
8 eggs
3 tablespoons finely chopped
    flat-leaf parsley
chargrilled bread, to serve

Translating Arabic to English can be tricky. That is why, in the world of food, you often see the names of Middle Eastern dishes spelled in different ways, as with this fabulously flavorsome dish from North Africa.

This must be the vegetarian equivalent to bacon and eggs as hangover food. The name alone makes you want to sit up and take notice.

Preheat the grill to high.

Put the oil in a large bowl. Add the tomatoes, bell peppers, and onion and toss the vegetables around to coat them in the oil.

Working in batches, tumble some of the vegetables over the grill and spread them around so they don't overlap. Cook the vegetables for 8–10 minutes, turning them often using metal tongs until they are tender and scored with grill marks, then transfer to a bowl. Cook the remaining vegetables in the same way.

Sprinkle the cooked vegetables with the chile, cumin, paprika, and salt and toss together. Lightly mash using a potato masher, so the tomatoes especially are well crushed. Spoon the mixture onto a heavy-bottomed baking tray. Put the tray on the grill and allow to heat up and sizzle.

Form eight evenly spaced little wells in the mixture, then crack an egg into each one.

Close the grill lid, if your grill has one, or place another baking tray over the top. Cook for 8–10 minutes, just until the egg whites are firm. Sprinkle with the parsley and serve hot, with chargrilled bread.

VEGETARIAN BARBECUE

MUSHROOMS WITH MANCHEGO RAREBIT

Serves 4

Manchego is a Spanish cheese, not unlike cheddar. This dish is a hybrid of a fondue and Welsh rarebit. Again, as with the other mushroom recipes, feel free to substitute other varieties — so long as they're not tiny!

½ cup beer
2 cups grated manchego cheese
olive oil, for brushing
12 medium-sized field mushrooms
flat-leaf parsley sprigs, to garnish
smoked paprika, for sprinkling

Preheat the grill hotplate to medium.

Combine the beer and cheese in a small saucepan. Cook over medium heat, stirring until the mixture is smooth. Sit the saucepan on a warm part of the grill to keep the mixture gooey.

Lay a sheet of parchment paper on the hotplate and lightly brush with olive oil to grease it. Sit the mushrooms, gill side down, on the parchment paper. Cook for 8–10 minutes, or until tender.

Turn the mushrooms over, then spoon the rarebit into the caps. Close the grill lid, or cover the mushrooms with a baking tray. Cook for 5 minutes, until the cheese has melted and the mushrooms are tender.

Serve hot, garnished with parsley, and sprinkled with paprika.

SIDES & SALADS

These recipes are about flavor and color. And lots of it. Side dishes and salads might be considered support acts, but occasionally they can be called upon to star as a starter dish.

Few things are better than sliced summer tomatoes splashed with olive oil and sea salt. But this is a grill recipe book, after all, and as much as I love a simple tomato salad, I also love using a grill to cook food.

The grill is used year round in my house. Rain is about the only thing to stop me, but even then I am lucky enough to have a large, sheltered porch from which to grill.

And year-round grilling means that non-summer vegetables are not overlooked. So, I make the most of late summer eggplant, beans in spring, root vegetables and leeks in fall. Even grilled fruits like figs and peaches can make a sweet salad addition when tossed with some bitter lettuce leaves, nuts, and cheese.

Have a tangy, vinegar-spiked dressing on hand to douse over hot grilled vegetables so they soak up all that flavor. Remember, salads aren't just for summer. Rug up in the cooler months and enjoy some hearty and comforting vegetables, hot off the grill.

GRILLED CAULIFLOWER WITH VINEGAR & GARLIC DRESSING

Serves 4–6

---

1 small cauliflower,
   about 2 lb 4 oz
2 tablespoons rice bran oil

VINEGAR & GARLIC DRESSING
1 tablespoon finely chopped
   garlic
¼ cup light olive oil
1 teaspoon smoked Spanish
   paprika
½ cup roughly chopped flat-leaf
   parsley
1 teaspoon sea salt
¼ cup red wine vinegar

If you are thinking it is odd to cook cauliflower on the grill then I would have to agree. I'm no huge fan of cooking "hard" vegetables on the grill, but the method used here works nicely. The cauliflower is first parboiled, rendering it tender. The grill then heats it up just enough to warmly bring out all the flavors of the Spanish-inspired dressing.

To make the dressing, put the garlic in a heatproof bowl. Heat the olive oil in a small saucepan over high heat. When smoking hot, pour the oil over the garlic so it sizzles, softens, and infuses the oil. Before the garlic browns, quickly stir in the paprika, parsley, and salt, then add the vinegar. Set aside to infuse.

Cut the cauliflower into large florets, then in half lengthways. Bring a large saucepan of water to a boil and add the cauliflower. When the water returns to the boil, remove the pan from the heat and drain the cauliflower well. Toss the cauliflower in a large bowl with the rice bran oil and a little sea salt.

Preheat the grill or hotplate to high. Tumble the cauliflower over the grill and cook for 2–3 minutes on each side, or until lightly golden.

Return the cauliflower to the bowl and pour the dressing over. Leave for at least 30 minutes for the tasty flavors to infuse the cauliflower, turning occasionally.

Turn the cauliflower in the dressing again before serving.

**VEGETARIAN
BARBECUE**

ISRAELI EGGPLANT SALAD

If you're ever looking for a decent reference book on cooking vegetables, try to get your hands on a copy of Mollie Katzen's *The Enchanted Broccoli Forest*. In the eighties it was in the kitchen of just about every other student. It is a well-worn book on my shelf and was the inspiration for this delicious recipe.

Preheat the grill to high.

Sit the eggplants and tomatoes on the grill. When they start to smoke, give them a turn. Continue until the vegetables look charred all over, then remove from the grill.

When cool enough to handle, peel the eggplant skins and discard — there's no need to be too fussy about removing all the burnt bits as these add flavor. Tear the flesh of the eggplant into long lengths and place in a bowl.

Peel and discard the skins of the tomatoes. Chop the flesh and add it to the eggplant, along with any seeds and juice. Don't mix them together at this stage.

Put the dressing ingredients in a bowl and stir to combine. Pour the dressing over the vegetables and use a large spoon to gently coat all the vegetables — you don't want to break them up too much. Stir the herbs through and season well.

Serve warm, or at room temperature, garnished with extra parsley.

2 eggplants
4 truss tomatoes
1 cup cilantro leaves
1 cup chopped flat-leaf parsley, plus extra leaves, to garnish

DRESSING
¼ cup olive oil
¼ cup lemon juice
2 teaspoons ground cumin
2 teaspoons hot paprika
½ teaspoon cayenne pepper

SIDES & SALADS

SWEET & SOUR SQUASH

Serves 6

1 small winter squash
2 tablespoons rice bran oil

DRESSING
⅓ cup red wine vinegar
¼ cup olive oil
2 garlic cloves, finely chopped
¼ teaspoon chile flakes
2 teaspoons soft brown sugar
1 cup mint leaves, roughly
    chopped
¼ cup currants

Sweet and sour is not a flavor combination unique to Chinese cooking. The Sicilians are masters too, albeit in a much more subtle way. The combination of sugar and vinegar is common in southern Italian cooking.

Cut the squash in half using a large knife. Scoop out the seeds with a large metal spoon and discard. Lay the cut side of the squash flat on a chopping board. Cut the squash into thick wedges, following the natural indentations.

Place the squash in a bowl with the rice bran oil, season well with sea salt and freshly ground black pepper, and toss to coat.

Combine the dressing ingredients in a bowl, mix well to dissolve the sugar, then set aside.

Preheat the grill hotplate to medium.

Lay the squash wedges on the hotplate, cut side down, and cook for 10 minutes. Turn the squash over and cook for another 5–10 minutes, until just tender — you want the squash pieces to retain some firmness so they don't break up too much.

Place the hot squash in a large bowl. Pour the dressing over, toss to combine, then season to taste.

Serve warm, or at room temperature.

112

VEGETARIAN BARBECUE

FIG SKEWERS WITH ARUGULA, PARMESAN, & POMEGRANATE SALAD

Serves 4

2 cups baby arugula leaves
2 tablespoons extra virgin
   olive oil
8 firm, ripe figs
1 tablespoon pomegranate
   molasses
½ cup shaved Parmesan cheese
3 tablespoons fresh
   pomegranate seeds
2 lemons, cut into
   slices 1¼ inches thick

Figs come and go, which is what makes them so special. I have tried all sorts of tasty treats with figs this season.

As a sweet treat, I serve ripe figs with sweetened, orange-flavored mascarpone, with almonds and organic honey. For a savory option, simply halve, skewer, and chargrill the figs and top with light shavings of good Parmesan cheese.

Soak four bamboo skewers in cold water for 30 minutes.

Preheat the grill to high.

Toss the arugula and olive oil in a bowl and season to taste with sea salt and freshly ground black pepper. Scatter the arugula on a serving plate.

Cut the figs in half and thread four halves onto each skewer. Brush the figs with the pomegranate molasses. Spread the skewers on the grill and cook for 5–6 minutes, turning often, until golden and caramelized.

Arrange the skewers on a large serving plate. Top with the Parmesan and pomegranate seeds.

Serve warm, with the lemon slices for squeezing over.

114

VEGETARIAN BARBECUE

THE MUST-HAVE GRILLED VEGETABLE SALAD

Serves 8

This is a very simple, very tasty recipe to have in your repertoire. Start with a few basics: Chopped garlic, chile, parsley, some sort of oil, and something with a tang factor (like vinegar or lemon juice), then just add whatever grilled vegetables you like.

In summer I am partial to vine vegetables — eggplant, tomatoes, and beans.

Combine the dressing ingredients in a bowl and set aside to infuse.

Preheat the grill hotplate and grill to high.

Tumble the tomatoes over the hotplate — avoid cooking them on the grill as they will stick. Spread the eggplant around the grill. Depending on the size of your grill, you may need to cook the vegetables in batches. Don't overcrowd the grill, and make sure the vegetables don't overlap — they'll cook better this way. Keep turning the vegetables until they are tender and golden.

Put the cooked vegetables in a large bowl. While they're still warm, spoon some of the dressing over them, but don't stir the vegetables or they'll break up.

Cook the beans and onions on the grill in the same manner. When all the vegetables are cooked and in the bowl, pour the remaining dressing over.

Tip the salad onto a serving platter. Serve at room temperature.

2 lb 4 oz plum tomatoes, halved lengthways
2 large eggplants, cut into large chunks
1 lb 2 oz green beans
2 red onions, cut into thin rings

DRESSING
4 garlic cloves, finely chopped
2 large red chiles, finely chopped
1 cup roughly chopped flat-leaf parsley
½ cup olive oil
¼ cup sherry vinegar
1 teaspoon sea salt

115

SIDES & SALADS

TANGY SWEET POTATO SALAD

Serves 4

There are some ingredients that, when used with a light hand, give warmth to a dish. Caraway is one of them. Use it sparingly, like fennel seeds, and you will be left wondering what the flavor is exactly. But it doesn't matter, it just tastes very good.

1 medium-sized sweet potato,
   sliced into rounds
   ¼ inch thick
2 tablespoons rice bran oil
1 teaspoon caraway seeds
2 dill pickles, finely chopped
3 tablespoons roughly chopped
   mint leaves
1 large red chile, finely chopped
2 tablespoons apple cider
   vinegar
¼ cup extra virgin olive oil
1 teaspoon superfine sugar

Preheat the grill to medium.

Put the sweet potato, rice bran oil, and caraway seeds in a bowl and toss to coat the sweet potato well.

Tumble the sweet potato over the grill, then use tongs to spread them out so they don't overlap. Cook for 8–10 minutes on each side, or until caramelized and tender.

Place the hot sweet potato in a bowl. Add the dill pickles, mint, and chile. In a small bowl, combine the vinegar, olive oil, and sugar, then drizzle the mixture over the sweet potatoes, gently stirring to combine. Set aside for 30 minutes for the flavors to infuse.

Season to taste with sea salt and freshly ground black pepper and serve.

SPICED PARSNIPS

Serves 4–6

3 tablespoons light olive oil
1 teaspoon ground turmeric
1 teaspoon fennel seeds
1 teaspoon cumin seeds
¼ teaspoon chile powder
1 teaspoon sea salt
2 lb 4 oz medium-sized parsnips
3 tablespoons torn mint leaves
lemon wedges, to serve

Parsnips may seem an odd thing to grill, but I grill them in winter, when they are abundant and well priced. This vegetable needs to be parboiled beforehand, otherwise it will burn before it is cooked through.

In a large bowl, combine the olive oil, turmeric, fennel seeds, cumin seeds, chile powder, and salt.

Bring a saucepan of water to the boil. Peel the parsnips and cut in half lengthways, then add them to the boiling water and cook for 4–5 minutes, or until just starting to soften. Drain well.

Tip the warm parsnips into the bowl with the spiced oil and toss to coat. Cover and set aside at room temperature for 1 hour.

Preheat the grill hotplate to high.

Keeping the bowl near the grill, lift the parsnips out, letting the excess spiced oil drip back into the bowl, and reserving the spiced oil. Tumble the parsnips over the hotplate and spread them out so they don't overlap.

Cook the parsnips for 5 minutes on each side, or until tender and slightly charred. Drizzle the reserved spiced oil over the parsnips and cook for just a few more seconds.

Transfer to a serving plate and season with sea salt and freshly ground black pepper to taste. Scatter with the mint.

Serve warm, with lemon wedges.

**VEGETARIAN
BARBECUE**

BOLD POTATOES

Serves 4

Those who know even a little Spanish will probably recognize this as patatas bravas, a much bastardized dish. Potatoes are not supposed to be eaten cold and wrinkled. Cold is fine, but not wrinkled too, which is how this dish is done by the lazy chef — even though it is actually less effort to make these splendid potatoes live up to their name.

These are very good enjoyed with a glass of rosé or some Spanish beer.

Combine the sauce ingredients in a bowl. Season to taste with sea salt and freshly ground black pepper. Cover and set aside for the flavors to develop while cooking the potatoes.

Preheat the grill hotplate to medium.

Cut the potatoes into slices no thicker than ¼ inch. Place in a bowl, add 1 tablespoon of the olive oil and the salt, then toss around to evenly coat the slices in the oil.

Tumble the potatoes over the hotplate and use tongs to spread the slices out so they don't overlap. Close the lid, if your grill has one, and cook for 10 minutes, or until golden. (If your grill doesn't have a lid, just cook the potatoes a little longer at a slightly lower temperature.)

Turn the potato slices over, close the lid and cook for another 5–6 minutes, or until golden and tender.

Spread the sauce down the middle of a long serving plate. Tumble the potatoes over, scatter with the parsley, and drizzle with the remaining olive oil. Serve hot.

4 large boiling potatoes,
    scrubbed but not peeled
¼ cup olive oil
1 teaspoon sea salt
1 cup roughly chopped flat-leaf
    parsley

SAUCE
1 cup puréed tomatoes
⅓ cup good-quality mayonnaise
2 garlic cloves, crushed
2 tablespoons white wine vinegar
1 teaspoon smoked paprika
1 teaspoon ground cumin
1 teaspoon chile flakes

POOR MAN'S POTATOES

Serves 6–8

2 lb 4 oz new potatoes, cut in half
2 red onions, thickly sliced
2 green bell peppers,
    thickly sliced
4 garlic cloves, finely sliced
2 bay leaves
3 tablespoons roughly chopped
    flat-leaf parsley
¼ cup olive oil
¼ cup white wine
1 teaspoon smoked paprika
1 teaspoon sea salt
good-quality mayonnaise,
    to serve

I love titles like this. They come from a time when people were so much more snobby and classist about who ate what. And if you ate potatoes you were considered poor! But how good are potatoes, fried into chips, mashed with cream, slow-cooked in a curry... or baked in foil with a few aromatics, as they are here.

Tear off two large sheets of foil, about 12 inches long. Tear off two sheets of parchment paper about the same size, then rinse the paper under cold water and wring out the excess water. The parchment paper will look like crumbled fabric. Lay the damp paper on the foil.

Preheat the grill hotplate to medium. Close the lid of the grill to create a hot oven effect. (If your grill doesn't have a lid, simply cook the potatoes at a lower temperature, and for slightly longer than the times given below.)

Put all the ingredients, except the mayonnaise, in a clean plastic bag. Hold the bag shut and shake vigorously to make sure all the ingredients are really well combined. Tumble the contents of the bag onto the parchment paper. Bring the edges of the foil together and twist to enclose the potato mixture, so it looks like a giant dumpling. Secure the foil with kitchen twine or wooden pegs.

Sit the foil bag on the grill, close the lid and cook for 20 minutes. Use a clean cloth to grab the top of the foil bag and gently shake so the flavors are well combined and coat the potatoes. Turn the bag over and cook for a further 15 minutes, or until the potatoes are tender.

Serve the potatoes warm or at room temperature, with a dollop of mayonnaise.

124

VEGETARIAN BARBECUE

LEMON SOY GRILLED ONIONS

Serves 4

Chargrilled onions smell so wonderfully appetizing when cooked on the grill. Onions may well be the vegetable that most people associate with grilled food! Here the humble onion is combined with some simple flavors for a super-tasty result.

4 white onions, thickly sliced
2 tablespoons rice bran oil
1 teaspoon sea salt
¼ cup tamari
   (Japanese soy sauce)
¼ cup lemon juice
1 tablespoon mirin
1 teaspoon shichimi togarashi
   (see Note)

Preheat the grill to high.

Put the onions and oil in a bowl and toss to coat. Tumble the onions over the grill and sprinkle with the salt. Use tongs to spread them around so the onions don't overlap. Cook, turning often, for 10–15 minutes, or until golden and tender.

Transfer the onions to a serving plate. Combine the soy sauce, lemon juice, and mirin in a bowl, then pour the mixture over the onions while they are still warm.

Sprinkle with the spice powder and serve.

NOTE: Also known as Japanese seven-spice, shichimi togarashi is a zesty spice mixture containing ground red chiles, sesame seeds, ginger, and seaweed, commonly sprinkled over soup, noodles, and fried foods. It's widely sold in Asian supermarkets and spice shops.

GRILLED CORN WITH HOT SALSA

Serves 4

4 fresh corn cobs
¼ cup melted butter
¼ cup finely grated
   Parmesan cheese

SALSA
2 tablespoons olive oil
1 tablespoon lime juice
3 tablespoons finely diced
   roasted piquillo peppers or
   red bell pepper
3 tablespoons chopped jalapeño
   chiles, in brine, drained
½ cup roughly chopped cilantro
   leaves and stalks
2 scallions, thinly sliced

I had a corn recipe in my original *Fired Up* grill book, which proved to be really popular. It involved serving grilled corn with butter, lime juice, and Parmesan cheese. Using Parmesan here may sound a little odd, but it really adds an extra savory element — something the Japanese call "umami."

Combine all the salsa ingredients in a large bowl and set aside.

Preheat the grill hotplate to high.

Brush the corn cobs with some of the melted butter, sit them on the hotplate, and cook for 8–10 minutes, turning and brushing with more melted butter every couple of minutes, until the corn is starting to char around the edges.

Transfer the corn cobs to a plate. Season well with salt and freshly ground black pepper and sprinkle with the Parmesan.

Serve warm, with the salsa on the side.

**VEGETARIAN
BARBECUE**

GRILLED EGGPLANT WITH CHIPOTLE LABNEH

Serves 4–6

Labneh is a slightly tangy, soft cheese made from salted and strained yogurt, widely enjoyed for breakfast in the Middle East. As it has increased in popularity it is much easier to get your hands on these days. Try it once and you will appreciate its deliciousness!

If you can't find labneh, don't despair: It is very easy to make yourself. For every cup of natural yogurt, stir through 1 teaspoon salt. Spoon it into some clean cloth, such as cheesecloth, and firmly tie to enclose the yogurt in the cloth. Suspend it over a bowl so the water drips out, then refrigerate overnight. The next day, have a look in the cloth and you will see labneh.

Put the chipotle labneh ingredients in a food processor and whiz until just combined, leaving some flecks of chile. Set aside.

Preheat the grill to high.

Cut the eggplant lengthways down the middle, then cut each piece crossways in half. Place in a bowl, drizzle with the rice bran oil, and toss to coat the eggplant.

Tumble the eggplant over the grill, using tongs to spread the pieces out so they don't overlap. Cook, turning often, for 10–15 minutes, or until golden all over.

Place the eggplant in a bowl. Add the garlic, lemon juice, and herbs and toss together while the eggplant is still hot.

Tumble the eggplant onto a serving plate. Drizzle with olive oil and serve with thick dollops of the chipotle labneh.

NOTE: Chipotle chiles are often packed in adobo — a spicy red chile sauce. You'll find them packed in cans and jars in spice shops and good food stores.

2 small eggplants,
    no more than 6 inches long
2 tablespoons rice bran oil
1 garlic clove, crushed
2 tablespoons lemon juice
3 tablespoons roughly chopped
    mint leaves
3 tablespoons roughly chopped
    flat-leaf parsley
extra virgin olive oil, for drizzling

CHIPOTLE LABNEH
2 whole smoked chipotle
    chiles in adobo sauce, plus
    1 tablespoon of the sauce
    (see Note)
10½ oz labneh

SICILIAN GRILLED VEGETABLE SALAD

Serves 4–6

2 medium-sized eggplants
1 small cauliflower
1 tablespoon light olive oil

DRESSING
½ cup olive oil
2 tablespoons red wine vinegar
2 garlic cloves, crushed
1 cup roughly chopped mint
1 cup roughly chopped flat-leaf
    parsley leaves
1 cup basil leaves, torn
2 tablespoons small salted
    capers, rinsed and drained
½ teaspoon sugar
¼ cup raisins

**I'm using eggplant and cauliflower here, but you could also use zucchini, broccolini, and bell pepper. Any vegetable will do, really, so long as you add the dressing to the
just-cooked vegetables, letting them soak up all the tasty bits — kind of like a reverse marinade.**

Combine all the dressing ingredients in a large bowl.

Preheat the grill to medium.

Slice the eggplants into ½ inch rounds, and cut the cauliflower into bite-sized florets. Put them in a bowl with the olive oil, season well with sea salt and freshly ground black pepper and toss to coat.

Tumble the eggplant and cauliflower over the grill and spread them out so they don't overlap. Cook for 8–10 minutes, then turn them over and cook for another 5 minutes, or until just tender.

Put the hot vegetables in a large bowl, pour the dressing over and toss to combine. Cover with plastic wrap and set aside at room temperature for at least 30 minutes or up to 1 hour, allowing all the flavors to infuse.

Toss together, season to taste and serve.

**VEGETARIAN
BARBECUE**

SUGAR SQUASH WITH LENTILS & TANGY DRESSING

Serves 4

It would not be the first or last time I have used the following technique to make a dressing or a sauce. Gently heating aromatics in some oil teases out the flavors and infuses these through the oil. And don't be afraid of lentils — they are tender, tasty, and good for you.

To make the dressing, put the olive oil, chile, and garlic in a small saucepan over medium heat. When the chile and garlic start to sizzle, cook for just a minute or two longer, then remove from the heat. Stir in the vinegar, sugar, and salt and mix until dissolved. Pour into a jar or bowl and set aside to infuse.

Put the lentils in a small saucepan and pour in enough water to cover. Bring to a boil, then reduce the heat and simmer until the lentils are tender but not mushy — this may take as little as 5 minutes, or up to 20 minutes, depending on the age of your lentils, so check them regularly. Drain well and set aside.

Preheat the grill to medium.

Cut the squash in half, then scoop out and discard the seeds. Leaving the skin on, cut the squash into wedges no thicker than ¾ inch. Brush the flesh with the rice bran oil and cook on the grill for 10 minutes on each side, or until golden and cooked through, checking regularly to ensure it doesn't burn too much.

Put the hot squash in a large bowl with the onion, herbs, and lentils. Stir the dressing, then pour it over the squash.

Toss gently to combine. Serve warm.

¼ cup puy lentils
   or tiny blue-green lentils
1 sugar or butternut squash,
   about 4 lb 8 oz
1 tablespoon rice bran oil
1 red onion, finely sliced
1 cup small mint leaves
1 cup flat-leaf parsley leaves

TANGY DRESSING
¼ cup light olive oil
1 large red chile, finely sliced
4 garlic cloves, finely sliced
¼ cup white wine vinegar
2 tablespoons sugar
½ teaspoon sea salt

133

SIDES & SALADS

INDIAN SPICED EGGPLANT

Serves 4–6

2 medium-sized eggplants
2 tablespoons rice bran oil
3 teaspoons sea salt
2 tablespoons olive oil
1 garlic clove, crushed
1 teaspoon ground cumin
½ teaspoon chile powder
½ cup labneh
    (strained yogurt cheese;
    see introductory notes on
    page 129)
1 cup mint leaves, roughly torn

Take note of this method of adding seasoning and flavor to just-cooked eggplant. The heat of the eggplant releases the fragrant oil in the spices. Eggplant is a highly absorbent vegetable — you'll notice how much oil it sucks up when being fried.

Preheat the grill to medium.

Cut the eggplants lengthways into large wedges. Place in a bowl with the rice bran oil and salt and toss to coat in the oil. Tumble the eggplant onto the grill and cook for 12–15 minutes, using tongs to spread the wedges out and to turn them often, until golden and just tender. Transfer to a bowl.

Combine the olive oil, garlic, cumin, and chile powder in a small bowl. Pour the dressing over the eggplant while it is still hot, then gently toss to coat in the spice mixture.

Pile the eggplant onto a serving platter. Serve warm, scattered with the mint, with the labneh on the side.

**VEGETARIAN
BARBECUE**

CHARGRILLED PANEER & SPINACH SALAD

Serves 4

What you're after here is the salad all ready to go in a bowl. To this you are going to toss through warm, golden, just-cooked cubes of paneer and a simple dressing. The warm paneer will soften the spinach and entice the flavors from the dressing.

Preheat the grill or hotplate to high.

Combine the spinach, tomatoes, scallions, and cilantro in a large bowl and set aside.

Pat the paneer dry with kitchen paper and cut into ¾ inch cubes. Place in a bowl, drizzle with a little olive oil and toss to coat. Put the paneer cubes on the grill or hotplate and cook for about 8 minutes, turning often so each side is golden.

Add the warm cheese to the spinach mixture, along with the cumin, olive oil, and lemon juice. Season to taste with sea salt and freshly ground black pepper and toss to combine.

Serve the salad while the cheese is still warm.

7 oz baby English spinach leaves

7 oz small teardrop tomatoes, halved

2 scallions, thinly sliced on an angle

½ cup roughly chopped cilantro leaves

7 oz block paneer (Indian cottage cheese; see introductory notes on pages 38 and 75)

2 tablespoons olive oil, plus extra for drizzling

1 teaspoon ground cumin

2 tablespoons lemon juice

139

SIDES & SALADS

BALINESE GRILLED EGGPLANT WITH TOMATO SAMBAL

Serves 4

2 eggplants
vegetable oil, for brushing
lime wedges, to serve

SAMBAL
4 ripe tomatoes
4 garlic cloves, unpeeled
2 red Asian shallots, unpeeled
1 vegetable broth cube,
    preferably gluten free
1 small red chile
¼ teaspoon ground white pepper
2 tablespoons soft brown sugar

Sambal is to Bali and Indonesia what harissa is to Morocco. This is an unadulterated chile sauce — hot, spicy, and with a real kick. It is added to curries and used as a condiment in its own right with grilled meats.

Preheat the grill to high.

To make the sambal, sit the tomatoes, garlic, and shallots on the grill and cook for 8–10 minutes, turning often and removing each vegetable from the grill when they are charred all over. Remove from the heat until cool enough to handle, then peel all the vegetables and discard the skins.

Put the garlic flesh in a food processor with the tomatoes, shallots, crumbled broth cube, chile, pepper, and sugar. Whiz together until smooth, then pour the mixture into a small saucepan and simmer for 10 minutes, or until slightly thickened. Transfer to a bowl and allow to cool.

Preheat the grill to medium.

Cut each eggplant in half lengthways and make several shallow, diagonal incisions on the flesh side of the eggplant. Brush the cut side with oil. Place on the grill, cut side down, and cook for 8–10 minutes, or until golden and charred around the edges.

Turn the eggplant over and cook for another 5 minutes, or until it has collapsed and is soft.

Serve the eggplant warm, with some sambal spooned over, and lime wedges on the side.

140

VEGETARIAN BARBECUE

CHARGRILLED FENNEL WITH CHILE & HERBS

Serves 4

Fennel in all its forms is delicious. The feathery tops add flavor to dressings and mayonnaise. The beefy bulbs can be cooked in all sorts of ways — in pasta sauces, risotto, minestrone, and roasted with pork or chicken. Fennel seeds are a staple in my cupboard, ready to be used in Indian and Italian-inspired recipes.

4 medium-sized fennel bulbs,
   preferably with fronds
2 garlic cloves, chopped
3 tablespoons olive oil
2 tablespoons red wine vinegar
2 teaspoons dijon mustard
½ teaspoon sea salt
dried chile flakes, to taste
1 cup flat-leaf parsley
   leaves, finely chopped
1 cup mint leaves, finely chopped

If the fennel has feathery fronds, cut these off and roughly chop up enough to give a small handful. Set aside.

Slice the fennel lengthways into slices ¼ inch thick. Place in a bowl with the garlic and 1 tablespoon of the olive oil. Set aside at room temperature for 30 minutes to infuse.

In a large bowl, combine the remaining olive oil with the remaining ingredients to make a herb dressing.

Preheat the grill to high.

Tumble half the fennel over the grill and spread the slices out so they don't overlap. Cook for 4–5 minutes on each side, until the fennel is golden and charred and the garlic is golden and aromatic. Add the hot fennel to the herb dressing and toss to coat.

Cook the remaining fennel in the same manner and toss it through the dressing. Serve warm or at room temperature, sprinkled with any reserved fennel fronds.

143

SIDES & SALADS

GRILLED BEANS WITH MISO DRESSING

Serves 4

10½ oz green beans
1 tablespoon rice bran oil
½ teaspoon black sesame seeds

MISO DRESSING
3 tablespoons white miso
1 teaspoon superfine sugar
2 tablespoons sake
1 teaspoon tamari (Japanese soy
    sauce) or light soy sauce
½ teaspoon sesame oil

Beans are seasonal, which makes them extra special. They are pricey when sold pre-packed in small portions at the local supermarket. If you venture out to a farmers' market you will pick up a box of them for a fraction of the price. This miso dressing is great with grilled eggplant too.

You can trim any woody ends off the beans, but I prefer to leave them intact.

Place all the miso dressing ingredients in a food processor and whiz to combine. With the motor running, add ¼ cup hot water, so the mixture turns paler and more creamy in color. Set aside while cooking the beans.

Preheat the grill hotplate to high.

Toss the beans in a bowl with the oil until lightly coated.

Tumble the beans over the hotplate, then use tongs to spread them out so they don't overlap. Cook for 4–5 minutes, turning every minute or so, until the beans are nicely browned and tender around the edge.

Pile the beans into a bowl and sprinkle with the sesame seeds. Spoon the miso dressing over, or serve it on the side.

VEGETARIAN BARBECUE

CHARGRILLED LEEKS WITH HOT MUSTARD MISO DRESSING

Serves 4

It's best to use baby leeks here if you can, simply because they are novel and very seasonal. Otherwise, the big guys will do, but they will need longer on the grill and they may need a good bath beforehand.

16 baby leeks, untrimmed
2 tablespoons rice bran oil
1 teaspoon sea salt
2 teaspoons toasted sesame seeds

HOT MUSTARD MISO DRESSING
2 tablespoons white miso paste
2 teaspoons hot English mustard
2 tablespoons tamari (Japanese soy sauce)
2 tablespoons rice vinegar

Preheat the grill to high.

Wash the leeks well to remove any dirt from the roots. Rinse and drain well, then place the leeks on a tray. Add the oil and salt and toss to coat well.

Combine the dressing ingredients in a small bowl, using a fork to mash the miso and to whisk together until lump-free.

Cook the leeks on the grill for 8–10 minutes, or until golden and tender, turning them every now and then.

Lay the leeks on a serving plate and pour the dressing over. Serve warm, sprinkled with the sesame seeds.

POTATOES IN FOIL WITH HERBED LABNEH

Serves 4

4 large potatoes, with skin on, washed

HERBED LABNEH
½ cup labneh
1 tablespoon finely snipped chives
1 tablespoon finely chopped flat-leaf parsley
1 tablespoon finely chopped mint

Go and get some labneh (see introductory note on page 129) and try it, please. And use it in all kinds of dishes, as a substitute for all sorts of other things. Try it in dips instead of sour cream. Use it as you would hummus — or yogurt, which is what it is anyway. You can even use labneh to replace ricotta or cream cheese in sweets such as cheesecake.

Combine the ingredients for the herbed labneh in a bowl and mix together well. Cover and set aside at room temperature, or refrigerate until needed.

Preheat the grill hotplate to medium.

Wrap each potato in foil. Sit them on the hotplate, then close the grill lid, or cover the potatoes with a large stainless steel bowl or baking tray. Cook for 1 hour, turning often, until the potatoes are tender. You can check if the potatoes are cooked without unwrapping them by pressing on them with tongs or a spatula — when cooked, the potatoes will feel soft.

Remove the potatoes from the hotplate and leave them in their foil wrapping for 10–15 minutes. (You can leave them on the grill lid to keep warm.)

Unwrap the potatoes, then press down on them with a spatula to flatten and split the skin.

Spoon the herbed labneh over the hot potatoes and serve.

CHARGRILLED ASPARAGUS WITH DILL & MUSTARD CRÈME FRAÎCHE

Serves 4

This is not reinventing the wheel. Take one tasty, seasonally fresh vegetable — namely, asparagus — cook it simply, then combine it with other tasty classic ingredients. Do choose asparagus when it is in season, and please avoid buying asparagus that has flown a long way on a plane to reach you. That seems just too weird.

Preheat the grill to high.

Combine all the dill and mustard crème fraîche ingredients in a bowl. Mix together well and set aside.

Snap off and discard the woody ends of the asparagus. Toss the asparagus in a bowl with the olive oil and salt.

Tumble the asparagus over the grill and use tongs to spread the spears out so they don't overlap. Cook, turning often, for 6–8 minutes, or until lightly charred and tender.

Spread the dill and mustard crème fraîche over a large serving platter. Arrange the asparagus on top. Drizzle with olive oil and serve immediately.

24 thin asparagus spears
1 tablespoon light olive oil
½ teaspoon sea salt
extra virgin olive oil, for drizzling

DILL & MUSTARD
CRÈME FRAÎCHE
1 cup crème fraîche
2 tablespoons good-quality
    whole-egg mayonnaise
2 teaspoons dijon mustard
2 tablespoons finely chopped dill
2 tablespoons finely chopped
    flat-leaf parsley
1 tablespoon lemon juice

151

SIDES & SALADS

MIGAS & TOMATO SALAD

Serves 4

¼ cup milk
4 slices ciabatta bread
olive oil, for drizzling
3 tomatoes, roughly chopped
2 tablespoons red wine vinegar
1 small garlic clove, crushed
½ cup roughly chopped
   flat-leaf parsley

I'll interpret this in a very broad sense: Migas is a dish using leftover bread in Spanish, Portuguese, and Mexican cooking. The bread can be soaked in a mixture of milk and water and it is then deep-fried. This is a tasty technique, but impossible to replicate when cooking outside on a grill. Cooking the soaked bread on a hotplate is a convenient alternative, if not a bit healthier.

Preheat the grill hotplate to high.

Combine the milk and ¼ cup water in a bowl. Soak each slice of bread in this mixture for 1 minute.

Remove the bread from the milk mixture and gently squeeze out as much liquid as possible. Drizzle the hotplate generously with olive oil and cook the bread for a couple of minutes on each side, until golden and crispy around the edges.

Remove the bread from the hotplate and allow to cool. When cool enough to handle, roughly tear the bread and place in a bowl with the tomato, vinegar, garlic, and parsley. Season well with salt and freshly ground black pepper and gently toss to combine.

Serve warm.

**VEGETARIAN
BARBECUE**

SWEET POTATOES IN JACKETS WITH CREAMY FETA

Serves 4

Sweet potato, like potato, cooks up really well on the grill, wrapped in foil and cooked until fluffy and soft on the inside, with the skin a little chewy and sweet.

1 large sweet potato, peeled
⅓ cup olive oil
1 teaspoon sea salt

FETA & DILL CREAM
3½ oz soft feta cheese, crumbled
1 garlic clove, crushed
3 tablespoons chopped dill
2 tablespoons olive oil
2 tablespoons milk

To make the feta and dill cream, put the feta, garlic, dill, and olive oil in a food processor and whiz to a thick paste. With the motor running, add the milk, blending until thick and creamy. Set aside.

Cut the pointy ends off the sweet potato, then cut it into four portions about the same size.

Preheat the grill hotplate to medium.

Tear off four sheets of foil, large enough to completely wrap each piece of sweet potato. Sit a piece of sweet potato in the center of each piece of foil. Pour 1 tablespoon of the olive oil over each and sprinkle with the salt. Loosely wrap each portion in the foil and place them on the hotplate.

Close the grill lid, or cover the parcels with a baking tray. Cook for 45 minutes, turning often, until the sweet potato is very tender.

Unwrap the sweet potato parcels and spoon the feta and dill cream over while still hot.

CHARGRILLED CHICKORY WITH PARSLEY, LEMON, & PECORINO

Serves 4

light olive oil, for brushing
8 chicory, cut in half lengthways
1 teaspoon sea salt
1 cup roughly chopped flat-leaf
   parsley
2 tablespoons lemon juice
2 tablespoons finely shredded
   pecorino cheese

This recipe may well epitomize many of the great things about grilling, as well as many of the great things we associate with rustic, Italian cooking. Take a raw ingredient and don't mess with it too much — just grill until golden, sweet, and slightly charred, and serve with some herbs, lemon juice, and cheese. Nice.

Preheat the grill hotplate to medium–high and lightly brush with olive oil.

Sit the chicory, cut side up, on the hotplate. Cook for 5 minutes, or until golden underneath. Turn the chicory over and cook for another 5 minutes, or until tender.

Put the hot chicory in a large bowl with the remaining ingredients. Season with freshly ground black pepper and toss to combine.

Serve warm.

BREADS

When serving bread at a cookout, I prefer those that are best for sharing. In saying this, I realize that any bread can be broken as a symbol for sharing. But with a cookout I like to serve up breads that literally need to be broken, or torn, to be shared. This is pass-around bread. Break-with-your-hands bread. Scoop-up-something-tasty-with-it bread.

This sort of bread also has the added benefit of avoiding a knife and a chopping board. One less thing to remember when grilling is always a good thing.

For these breads I look to Asia, North Africa, the Mediterranean, and the Middle East for inspiration. From these places come the flatbreads, pan breads, or grilled breads that go best with my style of grilling.

These breads can be prepared in very little time, with very little fuss, and with very little knowledge of breadmaking. The traditions and techniques of these breads do not come from artisan bakers, chefs, or apprentices, but from homes and homemakers — from family cooks with very basic means, armed only with a pair of hands, a domestic oven, and a need to satisfy hunger.

Aside from making bread with ease, I think the most exciting element to these bread recipes is that you end up with something someone else is also enjoying in a place very different from you.

Using ingredients that can be found at any corner store, you can make bread that can be found in the piazzas of Sicily, the derbs of Marrakesh, the tapas bars of Spain, or dhabas of India. It's a very universal thing, bread. And these tasty, authentic breads are made to share, and can all be cooked on your very own grill.

PALERMO FOCACCIA

Makes 1 loaf

3 teaspoons instant dried yeast
3 cups bread flour,
    such as "00" flour
2 tablespoons olive oil, plus
extra
    for brushing
coarse polenta, for dusting
½ teaspoon sea salt
¼ cup puréed tomatoes
1 teaspoon dried oregano
extra virgin olive oil, to serve

There are many versions of this bread. This cake-like bread is a common staple in the market places of Palermo, Sicily. Sometimes anchovies are studded into the dough prior to baking, or fresh ricotta is smeared over the top. In situ, this bread looks more like a frosted cake. But do push this sweet simile aside: This is a really great-tasting, moreish bread.

Put ¼ cup warm water in a small bowl. Quickly stir in the yeast and 1 tablespoon of the flour, leaving the mixture lumpy. Cover and leave somewhere warmish and draught-free for 10–15 minutes, or until frothy and spongy-looking.

Brush a round metal baking pan with olive oil — my pan is 9 inches across and 2 inches deep. Sprinkle the base and sides with the polenta.

Put the salt and remaining flour in the bowl of an electric mixer fitted with a dough hook. Add the yeast mixture, olive oil, and 1 cup warm water and knead for 10 minutes, or until smooth and elastic. (Alternatively, mix the dough together, turn out onto a clean work surface and knead the dough by hand for 10 minutes.)

Tip the dough into the greased pan. Dip your fingers in flour and gently press the dough to the sides of the pan, making dimples as you go, and making sure it is an even thickness all over.

Spoon the tomatoes over the dough and sprinkle with the oregano. Leave in a warm, draught-free spot for about 1 hour, or until the dough has risen.

Preheat the grill to medium–high and close the lid to keep it warm. Put a rack on the grill and sit the focaccia pan on the rack. Close the lid, or cover the focaccia pan with a large stainless bowl. Cook for 15–18 minutes, or until the focaccia is golden around the edges and dry on top. (The bread may need longer cooking time if you are covering it with a bowl.)

Serve warm, with extra virgin olive oil for dipping into, and sea salt for sprinkling over.

VEGETARIAN BARBECUE

POCKET BREADS

Makes 8

These are fun. I am not sure how it actually works, but you end up with a puffed-up, disk-like bread. When cool, it can be split in two and used as a savory pocket — especially tasty when filled with falafel, hummus, pickled vegetables, and tangy tzatziki.

2¼ teaspoons instant dried yeast
1 teaspoon sugar
3⅓ cups bread flour,
    such as "00" flour,
    plus extra, for dusting
2 teaspoons sea salt

Pour ¼ cup warm water into a small bowl. Quickly stir in the yeast and sugar — leaving a few lumpy bits is fine. Cover and leave somewhere warmish and draught-free for 10–15 minutes, or until frothy and spongy-looking.

Put the flour and salt in a large bowl. Add the yeast mixture and 1 cup warm water and use one hand to combine. Tip the mixture onto a floured surface, or into the bowl of an electric mixer fitted with a dough hook. Knead for 15 minutes, or until the dough is smooth and elastic.

Divide the dough into eight equal portions. Shape each piece into a ball, then roll each ball into a disk about 4½–6 inches in diameter. Lay the disks on a sheet of floured parchment paper, then cover with a cloth and leave in a warm spot for about 1 hour, or until puffed and very soft.

Preheat the grill hotplate to high. Close the lid of the grill to allow the lid to get really hot.

Working in batches if necessary, put the pita breads on the hot grill lid and leave for 10 minutes. They will start to look dry and puff up, forming that distinctive pita or pocket-bread shape.

Turn the breads over and put them on a heavy-bottomed baking tray lined with parchment paper. Place a rack on the grill hotplate and place the tray of pita breads on top. (You may need to work in batches, depending on the size of your grill.) Close the lid and cook, turning often, for 5–8 minutes, or until golden and puffed.

The air inside the breads will be piping hot, so allow the breads to cool a little before serving.

161

FLATBREADS WITH PANEER & GREEN CHILE

Makes 8

2 cups all-purpose flour, plus
    extra, for dusting
½ teaspoon sea salt
1 teaspoon sugar
½ teaspoon baking soda
1¼ cups plain yogurt
2 tablespoons rice bran oil
lemon wedges, to serve

PANEER & GREEN
CHILE FILLING
1 small red onion, finely chopped
2 long green chiles, finely sliced
2 tablespoons finely chopped
    cilantro leaves and stalks,
    plus extra leaves, to garnish
3½ oz paneer (Indian cottage
    cheese; see introductory
    notes on pages 38 and 75),
    roughly shredded

It wasn't until I began researching recipes for this book that I realized how many varieties of bread are actually made in India — breads of different grains, both leavened and unleavened, with or without egg or dairy, oil, spices, and even with nuts. I wouldn't say no to any of them.

This bread is a type of kulcha, the sister of naan, made with baking soda rather than yeast. Both naan and kulcha can be served plain, or filled with whatever you like.

Combine the flour, salt, sugar, and baking soda in a bowl and make a well in the center. Add the yogurt to the well and use your hands to combine — the dough will be sticky and wet.

Make another well in the center and add the oil. Work the oil into the dough until the dough is smooth and shiny. Cover and set aside for 30 minutes, for the yogurt and soda to react.

Meanwhile, put the filling ingredients in a bowl and combine well.

Form the dough into eight balls, about the size of golf balls. On a lightly floured surface, roll each ball into a flat circle, about 4 inches across. Put one-eighth of the paneer mixture into the center of each, then bring the sides of the dough together to enclose the filling.

Again, on a lightly floured surface, roll each of the dough rounds into circles no thicker than ¼ inch. Place them on a lightly greased sheet of parchment paper, then cover with a cloth or plastic wrap. Set aside for about 30 minutes, or until slightly risen.

Preheat the grill hotplate to high. Close the lid to create an oven effect.

Using the parchment paper, lift the dough rounds onto the hotplate. Close the lid and cook for 3–4 minutes on each side, or until golden and cooked through.

Serve hot, with lemon wedges.

BARBARI BREAD

Makes 2 loaves

½ teaspoon sugar
2 teaspoons instant dried yeast
3¼ cups all-purpose flour
1 teaspoon sea salt
1 teaspoon baking soda
coarse polenta, for dusting
2 tablespoons sesame seeds

TOPPING
½ teaspoon all-purpose flour
½ teaspoon baking soda

This intriguing bread is the one most commonly eaten in Iran. Its distinctive elements are the parallel lines made in the dough prior to cooking, and the paste of flour, baking soda, and water that is brushed on top, creating a wonderfully crisp and dry bread. It is very nice with some feta cheese and olive oil.

Combine the sugar, yeast, and ¼ cup warm water in a small bowl. Cover and leave somewhere warmish and draught-free for 10–15 minutes, or until frothy and spongy-looking.

Mix the flour, salt, and baking soda together in a large bowl. Add the yeast mixture and 1¼ cups warm water and bring together into a sticky dough. Tip onto a floured board and knead for 15 minutes, or until smooth and elastic, or knead in an electric mixer with a dough hook for 10–15 minutes.

Divide the dough into two equal portions. Tear off two large sheets of parchment paper, about 16 inches long, and sprinkle with polenta. Place a piece of dough on each sheet, then shape each into a rectangle no more than ½ inch thick. Cover loosely with a cloth and set aside for about 1 hour.

Put the topping ingredients in a small saucepan with ⅓ cup water. Cook over medium heat for 1–2 minutes, or until the mixture is thick and cloudy. Allow to cool.

Preheat the grill hotplate to high. Sit a baking rack on the hotplate and close the grill lid.

Brush the liquid topping over each loaf. Use your fingers to run parallel divots, about ¾ inch apart, down the length of the dough. Sprinkle the sesame seeds over each loaf. Using the parchment paper, lift one of the loaves onto a baking tray, then sit the tray on the baking rack. Close the grill lid, reduce the heat to medium and cook for 10–15 minutes, or until the base of the bread is dark golden and the top is golden and dry.

Cook the remaining loaf in the same manner. Serve hot.

VEGETARIAN BARBECUE

AFGHANI FLATBREADS

Makes 2 loaves

These are big, rustic, easy-to-make breads. They are really another version of naan, with the option of making them bigger and thinner than the typical naan.

1 tablespoon instant dried yeast
5 cups all-purpose flour, plus
   extra for dusting
⅓ cup superfine sugar
1 tablespoon sea salt
¼ cup rice bran oil or grapeseed
   oil, plus extra for brushing

Combine the yeast and ¼ cup warm water in a small bowl. Cover and leave somewhere warmish and draught-free for 10–15 minutes, or until frothy and spongy-looking.

Put the flour, sugar, and salt into the bowl of an electric mixer fitted with a dough hook. With the motor running on low, add the yeast mixture, then add 3 cups warm water, then the oil. Knead for about 10 minutes, or until smooth and elastic. (Alternatively, mix the dough together, turn out onto a clean work surface and knead the dough by hand for 10 minutes.)

Put the dough in a large lightly oiled bowl. Cover and leave for about 1 hour, or until the dough has doubled in size and looks soft and pillow-like.

Divide the dough in half, then roll out each half on a well-floured work surface, into large, flat circles about 8 inches in diameter. Put the dough onto a lightly greased sheet of parchment paper, then use your fingers to press the dough all over, making dozens of little divots in the dough.

Preheat the grill hotplate to high. Put a baking rack on the hotplate. Use the parchment paper to lift one round of dough onto the baking rack. Close the lid of the grill to create an oven effect. (If your grill doesn't have a lid, cover the dough with a baking tray.) Cook for 10–15 minutes, or until the dough is golden. Brush the top side of the dough with a little oil, flip it over, then cover and cook for another 5 minutes, or until golden on both sides.

Cook the remaining dough in the same manner. Serve warm.

167

GRILLED GREEN OLIVE BREADS

Makes 4

This is a yeast-free "bread," and the basic recipe idea hails from northern China. Although, I must admit, the real inspiration comes from Barbara Tropp, a truly passionate and inspiring food writer. This recipe has the interesting technique of using hot and cold water to make the dough, combined with the "snail" shaping of the dough — resulting in a flaky, unleavened pastry.

Place the olive paste ingredients in a food processor and whiz until a smooth paste forms. Scrape into a bowl, then clean out the food processor bowl.

Put the flour and baking powder in the food processor and whiz to combine. With the motor running, add ⅓ cup boiling water, then ⅓ cup cold water. As soon as all the water has been added, turn the food processor off and scrape the dough out onto a floured surface.

Knead briefly, until the dough forms into a smooth ball. Cover and set aside at room temperature for about 30 minutes.

Divide the dough into four equal portions. Working one at a time, and leaving the others covered, roll out the dough on a lightly floured work surface, into a 8–10 inch circle. Spread one-quarter of the olive paste over the dough. Roll the dough up into a long, thin cigar shape, then coil the dough from one end to make a snail shape, tucking the end in. Repeat with the remaining dough and olive paste.

Now use a floured rolling pin to roll the snails into flat circles, about 6 inches across.

Preheat the grill hotplate to medium. (If you are cooking this bread on the grill rack, you will need to put it in the freezer until firm.)

Drizzle the oil over the hotplate, then sit one bread on top. Cook for 3–5 minutes on each side, turning every minute, until golden and slightly puffed. (If it starts to burn, reduce the temperature to medium–low.) Cook the remaining breads in the same way.

Serve hot, torn or cut into wedges.

2 cups all-purpose flour, plus
    extra for dusting
2 teaspoons baking powder
2 tablespoons rice bran oil

GREEN OLIVE PASTE
¼ cup olive oil
1 teaspoon sea salt
⅓ cup pitted large Sicilian
    green olives
1 garlic clove
½ cup chopped flat-leaf parsley
¼ cup sliced scallions

PIADINI STUFFED WITH MANCHEGO & PARSLEY

Serves 4

3 cups all-purpose flour
2 teaspoons sea salt
2 tablespoons Spanish vinegar
¼ cup extra virgin olive oil, plus extra, for brushing
5½ oz manchego cheese, coarsely shredded
4 tablespoons finely chopped flat-leaf parsley
1 small red onion, finely sliced
lemon wedges, to serve

Piadini is a type of unleavened Italian flatbread. Its rustic nature lends itself perfectly to rustic flavors: Onion, herbs, and hard cheeses.

Put the flour and salt in a food processor and whiz to combine. With the motor running, add the vinegar, oil, and enough cold water to bring the mixture together into large crumbs — you may need as little as 2 tablespoons cold water, or up to about 6 tablespoons.

Tip the mixture out onto a floured surface and knead for 8–10 minutes, until smooth. Wrap the dough in plastic wrap and set aside in a warmish place while you get everything else ready.

Combine the cheese, parsley, and onion in a bowl.

Preheat the grill hotplate to high.

Cut the dough into four even portions. Roll each dough portion on a floured surface into a long oval shape, about 16 inches long and 6 inches wide. Brush each round with olive oil.

Sprinkle the cheese mixture over two of the rounds, then top these with one of the other bread rounds to make a sandwich. Press the edges to seal them together.

Cook the piadini on the hotplate one at a time for 4–5 minutes, or until golden and crisp underneath. Flip the bread over and cook for another 3–4 minutes, or until golden.

Cut into wedges, or whatever shapes you prefer. Serve warm, with lemon wedges.

VEGETARIAN BARBECUE

REAL GARLIC BREAD

I say "real" garlic bread because I am using real ingredients here. Let me explain. The few times that I fine-dined as a kid in the seventies, I vaguely remember garlic bread being special. Now it is often something made with butter substitutes and garlic flakes. When made well, garlic bread is lovely. It is so easy to prepare ahead, ready to throw on the grill.

To make the garlic butter, put the garlic on a chopping board and sprinkle with the salt. Use a large knife to chop the garlic. Every now and then, use the flat side of the knife to press down on the chopped garlic to crush it even more. Continue until you have a very finely chopped heap of garlic. Stir the garlic and parsley through the butter.

Preheat the grill hotplate to medium. Sit a baking rack on the hotplate.

Cut deep slices into the bread, about ¾–1¼ inches apart. Spread the garlic butter into the cuts, making sure the exposed bread is evenly covered with the butter.

Completely wrap the bread in foil. Sit the bread on the baking rack, flat side down, and cook for 8–10 minutes.

Serve hot.

1 sourdough baguette, about 10–12 inches long

GARLIC BUTTER
6 organic garlic cloves
1 teaspoon sea salt
3 tablespoons finely chopped flat-leaf parsley
4½ oz organic unsalted/sweet butter, at room temperature

173

BREADS

DAMPER

Makes 1 loaf

2 cups all-purpose flour, plus
    extra for dusting
3 teaspoons baking powder
1 teaspoon sea salt
½ cup milk
olive oil, for brushing

This bread epitomizes Australian bush cookery. Like many good things, it originated out of necessity, created by stockmen on long journeys, from the most basic of ingredients. However, there's still a bit of an art to making damper — a bit like making scones. It might take a few attempts to get the damper looking "right," but it will always taste good.

Combine the flour, baking powder, and salt in a bowl, then make a deep well in the center.

In another bowl, combine the milk and ½ cup boiling water. Pour the mixture into the flour and use a fork to quickly combine for a few seconds. Now use one hand to mix the dough — it will be a wet dough, so you may need to add just a fine sprinkling of flour.

When the mixture no longer sticks to the side of the bowl, tip it out onto a lightly floured surface and knead for a minute, until smooth.

Using lightly oiled hands, form the dough into a log about 4 inches wide and 6 inches long.

Lay a large sheet of foil on a work surface and place a similar-sized sheet of parchment paper on top. Lightly brush the parchment paper with olive oil. Sit the dough at one long end of the parchment paper. Loosely roll the paper up, then fold the ends over to loosely enclose the dough. Set aside for 30 minutes.

Preheat the grill to medium.

Sit the bread on the grill and cook for 10 minutes. Turn it over and cook for another 10–13 minutes, or until the bread makes a hollow sound when tapped and is lightly golden all over.

Allow the damper to cool for a few minutes. Slice and serve while still warm.

**VEGETARIAN
BARBECUE**

NAAN

This Indian bread can be flavored with a whole bunch of ingredients: Nuts, dried fruit, herbs. But I like my naan unflavored so I can really appreciate its simplicity. What I most love to do with this bread is mop up any sauce left over from a curry.

1 teaspoon instant dried yeast
2 cups all-purpose flour, plus
　　extra for dusting
1 teaspoon superfine sugar
1 teaspoon sea salt
½ teaspoon baking powder
2 tablespoons rice bran oil, plus
　　extra for drizzling
¼ cup plain yogurt

Pour ¾ cup warm water into a bowl or jug and stir in the yeast. Set aside for a couple of minutes.

Combine the flour, sugar, salt, and baking powder in a large bowl. Add the oil and yogurt and combine with one hand. Add the yeast mixture and continue mixing with one hand to make a wet dough.

Lightly oil your hands, then form the dough into a ball. Place in a bowl, cover and set aside for 3–4 hours, or until the dough has doubled in size.

Lightly oil your hands again and divide the dough into six equal portions. Toss each one in flour to coat, then pull and stretch each piece on a lightly floured surface to make an oval shape about 8 inches long.

Preheat a grill to high. Sit a large heavy-bottomed baking tray on the grill and give it time to heat. Drizzle over some oil to lightly grease it.

Using an oven mitt, remove the tray from the grill, then carefully lay three of the naan breads on the hot tray. Use the flat side of a knife or the back of a spoon to press the dough into the tray. The dough will start cooking on the hot tray.

Sit the tray back on the hot grill and cook the breads for 4–5 minutes, or until the bread is crisp and golden underneath and the top is puffing up. Turn and cook for another 2–3 minutes, or until golden and cooked through. Keep the breads in a warm place.

Cook the remaining breads in the same manner. Serve warm.

175

BREADS

CORN GRIDDLE BREADS

Makes 4

1 cup all-purpose flour
2 teaspoons baking powder
¼ teaspoon sweet paprika,
    plus extra for sprinkling
½ teaspoon sea salt
1 egg, lightly beaten
¾ cup milk
½ cup creamed corn
2 tablespoons melted butter
vegetable oil, for brushing
good-quality mayonnaise,
    to serve
thinly sliced scallion, to serve

These could be called griddle cakes or even corn fritters. When these breads are kept very flat, I like to use them as I would any soft flatbread — they are soft enough to fold around grilled vegetables, or scoop up dips, sauces, and mayonnaise. Or you can top them with a simple fried egg or spicy Mexican beans. Yum.

Combine the flour, baking powder, paprika, and salt in a bowl, then make a well in the center.

In another bowl, combine the egg, milk, and creamed corn. Pour the mixture into the flour well with the melted butter and use a fork to combine.

Preheat the grill hotplate to medium and lightly brush with oil.

Pour or ladle the batter, using about ½ cup for each griddle bread, onto the hotplate, leaving room between each to expand. You should have enough batter for four griddle breads.

Use the back of the spoon to spread each one out into a circle about 4½–6 inches across. Cook for 4–5 minutes, or until bubbles form around the edges.

Flip them over and cook for another 2–3 minutes, or until golden and cooked through.

Serve warm, topped with a dollop of mayonnaise, some sliced scallion, and a sprinkling of paprika.

176

VEGETARIAN BARBECUE

INDEX

Page numbers in *italics* indicate photographs

179

VEGETARIAN BARBECUE

Vegetarian Barbecue
Text © Ross Dobson 2013
Design and Photography © Murdoch Books 2013
All rights reserved.

Published by HarperCollins Publishers Ltd

Originally published by Murdoch Books, an imprint of Allen & Unwin: 2013
First published in Canada by HarperCollins Publishers Ltd in this hardcover edition: 2014

The photographs on pages 26, 59, 60, 65, 74, 78, 90, 98, 104, 113, 121, 127, 131, 137, 142, 149, 155, 165 are by
Nicky Ryan, styling by Sarah O'Brien. All other photographs are by Brett Stevens, styling by Matt Page.

IMPORTANT: Those who might be at risk from the effects of salmonella poisoning (the elderly, pregnant
women, young children, and those suffering from immune deficiency diseases) should consult their doctor
with any concerns about eating raw eggs.

OVEN GUIDE: You may find cooking times vary depending on the oven you are using. For convection ovens,
as a general rule, set the oven temperature to 25°F lower than indicated in the recipe.

HarperCollins books may be purchased for educational, business, or sales promotional use through our
Special Markets Department.

HarperCollins Publishers Ltd
2 Bloor Street East, 20th Floor
Toronto, Ontario, Canada
M4W 1A8

www.harpercollins.ca

Library and Archives Canada Cataloging in Publication information is available upon request.

ISBN 978-1-44341-865-2

Designer: Hugh Ford
Photographers: Brett Stevens and Nicky Ryan
Stylists: Matt Page and Sarah O'Brien
Food Editor: Grace Campbell

Printed and bound in China
9 8 7 6 5 4 3 2 1